WOME
OF THE
WORD

BIBLE
STUDY
SERIES

BUILDING
BETTER
RELATIONSHIPS

BOBBIE YAGEL

Gospel Light

Published by Gospel Light
Ventura, California, U.S.A.
www.gospellight.com
Printed in the U.S.A.

Aglow International is an interdenominational organization of
Christian women. Our mission is to lead women to Jesus Christ and provide
opportunity for Christian women to grow in their faith and minister to others.
Our publications are used to help women find a personal relationship with
Jesus Christ, to enhance growth in their Christian experience, and to help them
recognize their roles and relationships according to Scripture. For more
information about our organization, please write to Aglow International,
P.O. Box 1749, Edmonds, WA 98020-1749, U.S.A., or call (425) 775-7282.
For ordering or information about the Aglow studies and other
resources, visit the Aglow E-store at www.aglow.org.

Rights for publishing this book outside the U.S.A. or in non-English languages are
administered by Gospel Light Worldwide, an international not-for-profit ministry.
For additional information, please visit www.glww.org, email info@glww.org, or write
to Gospel Light Worldwide, 1957 Eastman Avenue, Ventura, CA 93003, U.S.A.

To order copies of this book and other Gospel Light products in bulk quantities,
please contact us at 1-800-446-7735.

This book is dedicated to

*Myron, the love of my life, who graces me
with love and acceptance;*

*Our adult children: Craig, Stephen and Wendy,
constant sources of love, joy and pride;*

*Our daughter-in-law, Denise, and son-in-law, Jeff,
who fit so beautifully into our family;*

*Our grandchildren, Amber, Devin, Brandon and Daniel,
our delights, so easy to adore and cherish.*

CONTENTS

Foreword 7

Preface 9

Introduction..11

How to Start and Lead a Small Group 15

1. Building Right Relationships...17

2. Loving Our Neighbors 25

3. Honoring One Another...33

4. Encouraging One Another 45

5. Handling Confrontation 53

6. Befriending Our Emotions 63

7. Learning to Listen 75

8. Growing in Grace...83

Building Better Relationships Leader's Guide 97

OREWORD

When the apostle Paul poured out his heart in letters to the young churches in Asia, he was responding to his apostolic call to shepherd those tender flocks. They needed encouragement in their new life in Jesus. They needed solid doctrine. They needed truth from someone who had an intimate relationship with God and with them.

Did Paul know as he was writing that these simple letters would form the bulk of the New Testament? We can be confident that the Holy Spirit did! How like God to use Paul's relationship with these churches to cement His plan and purpose in their lives, and, generations later, in ours.

We in Aglow can relate to Paul's desire to bond those young churches together in the faith. After 1967, when Aglow fellowships began bubbling up across the United States and in other countries, they needed encouragement. They needed to know the fullness of who they were in Christ. They needed relationship. Like Paul, our desire to reach out and nurture from far away birthed a series of Bible studies that have fed thousands since 1973 when our first study, *Genesis*, was published. Our studies share heart-to-heart, giving Christians new insights about themselves and their relationship with and in God.

In 1998, God's generous nature provided us a rewarding new relationship with Gospel Light. Together we published our Aglow classics as well as a selection of exciting new studies. Gospel Light began as a publishing ministry much in the same way Aglow began publishing Bible studies. Henrietta Mears formed Gospel Light in response to requests from churches across America for the Sunday School materials she had written. Gospel Light remains a strong ministry-minded witness for the gospel around the world.

Our heart's desire is that these studies will continue to kindle the minds of women and men, touch their hearts, and refresh their spirits with the light and life a loving Savior abundantly supplies.

This study, *Building Better Relationships* by Bobbie Yagel, will show you how to develop and maintain relationships based on God's love and forgiveness. I know its contents will reward you richly.

Jane Hansen-Hoyt
International President
Aglow International

REFACE

The Bible describes two types of relationships: vertical and horizontal. John, the beloved disciple, best defined these when he wrote, "We love because he first loved us. If anyone says, 'I love God,' yet hates his brother, he is a liar. For anyone who does not love his brother, whom he has seen, cannot love God, whom he has not seen. And he has given us this command: Whoever loves God must also love his brother" (1 John 4:19-21).

In the fifth chapter of 1 John, the apostle rivets our attention to the interdependence of the love of God and the love of neighbor when he writes, "This is how we know that we love the children of God: by loving God and carrying out his commands" (1 John 5:2). Like the vertical and horizontal arms of the cross, our lives must illustrate a love for God and a love for others.

Our primary relationship is with God—all other relationships flow out from it. We must understand who we are in the Beloved—that God actually died to give us royal lineage and make us members of the family of heaven. When we truly accept this, believe this and become established in this truth, our security is in our relationship with Jesus Christ. Then, in the security of that relationship, we are empowered to reach out and build right relationships.

—Bobbie Yagel

INTRODUCTION

In the Bible, relationship rifts multiplied as fast as the earth's population: Adam and Eve refused to accept responsibility for their sin, blaming each other and the serpent; Cain murdered his brother, Abel, in a fit of jealous rage; Sarah mistreated and banished her slave Hagar; Jacob stole Esau's birthright and fled for his life; Laban cheated Jacob by giving him Leah for his wife instead of the promised Rachel; and Joseph's jealous brothers sold him into slavery. And these are only a few examples from the *first* book of the Bible.

The New Testament also reports relationship rifts: Jesus' disciples tried to outmaneuver each other for the place of honor at Jesus' side; doctrinal differences in the first-century Church erupted with an intensity that forced the disciples to call a conference in Jerusalem to settle escalating disputes; and Paul and Barnabas separated because of a disagreement over Mark's dependability as a missionary.

In light of these biblical examples, should we be surprised when our personal relationships sour? What we need to learn most of all is how to restore broken relationships and how to build right relationships.

Former Senate Chaplain Richard Halverson once described Christian fellowship as "coming together like grapes—crushed, with skins of ego broken, the ripe, fragrant juices of life mingling in the wine of sharing and understanding and caring." It sounds so good, so warm, so right—except that bit about the skins of ego being broken. Could the culprit of our relationship problems be the self that resists death?

Relationships are indeed the joy and the bane of the Christian life. In fellowship we receive support, encouragement, acceptance, help and love. But in fellowship we also experience rejection, judgment, discouragement, insensitivity and jealousy. Friends forsake us. Family members disappoint us. Gossip runs rampant in the Church. We are often reminded that the Christian Body is the only army that shoots its wounded. The Bible repeatedly reminds us that the only cure for damaged relationships is to love as Jesus loves us—unconditionally! This challenge strikes at the heart of where we live: in our homes, our neighborhoods, our churches and our places of employment.

This study tackles such nitty-gritty questions as: Do we talk with the person who is gossiping about us? Do we forgive those who refuse to ask for forgiveness or admit that they're wrong? How can we communicate with angry relatives without adding fuel to the fire?

Our relationships will be right to the extent that we take up our cross daily to die to self, grow in grace and let Christ be more fully formed in each of us. His ways bring healing, restore peace and promote love.

If your heart hungers after right relationships, you'll find the secrets in *Building Better Relationships*.

An Overview of the Study

This Bible study is divided into four sections:

1. *A Closer Look at the Problem* defines the problem and the goal of the lesson.

2. *A Closer Look at God's Truth* gets you into God's Word. What does God have to say about the problem? How can you begin to apply God's Word as you work through each lesson?

3. *A Closer Look at My Own Heart* will help you clarify and further apply biblical truths in your own life. It will also give guidance as you work toward change.

4. *Action Steps I Can Take Today* is designed to help you concentrate on immediate steps of action.

What You Will Need

· *A Bible*—The main Bible version used in this study is the *New International Version,* but you can use whatever Bible translation you are used to reading.

· *A Notebook*—During this study you will want to keep a journal to record what God shows you personally. You may also want to journal additional thoughts or feelings that come up as you go through the lessons. Some questions may require more space than is given in this study book.

- *Time to Meditate*—Only through meditation on what you're learning will you hear God's Word for you and begin to experience a heart knowledge, as well as a head knowledge, of the subject of building better relationships. Give the Holy Spirit time to personalize His Word to your heart so that you can know what your response should be to the knowledge you are gaining.

HOW TO START AND LEAD A SMALL GROUP

One key to leading a small group is to ask yourself, *What would Jesus do and how would He do it?* Jesus began His earthly ministry with a small group called the disciples, and the fact of His presence made wherever He was a safe place to be. Think of a small group as a safe place. It is a place that reflects God's heart and His hands. The way in which Jesus lived and worked with His disciples is a basic small-group model that we are able to draw both direction and nurture from.

Paul exhorted us to "walk in love, as Christ also has loved us and given Himself for us" (Ephesians 5:2, *NKJV*). We, as His earthly reflections, are privileged to walk in His footsteps, to help bind up the brokenhearted as He did or simply to listen with a compassionate heart. Whether you use this book as a Bible study, or as a focus point for a support group, a church group or a home group, walking in love means that we "bear one another's burdens" (Galatians 6:2, *NKJV*). The loving atmosphere provided by a small group can nourish, sustain and lift us up as nothing else can.

Jesus walked in love and spoke from an honest heart. In His endless well of compassion He never misplaced truth. Rather, He surrounded it with mercy. Those who left His presence felt good about themselves because Jesus used truth to point them in the right direction for their lives. When He spoke about the sinful woman who washed Jesus' feet with her tears and wiped them with her hair, He did not deny her sin. He said, "Her sins, which are many, are forgiven, for she loved much" (Luke 7:47, *NKJV*). That's honesty without condemnation.

Jesus was a model of servant leadership (see Mark 10:43-44). One of the key skills a group leader possesses is the ability to be an encourager of the group's members to grow spiritually. Keeping in personal contact with each member of the group, especially if one is absent, tells each one that he or she is important to the group. Other skills an effective group leader demonstrates include being a good listener, guiding the discussion, as well as guiding the group to deal with any conflicts that arise within it.

Whether you're a veteran or brand new to small-group leadership, virtually every group you lead will be different in personality and dynamic. The constant is the presence of Jesus Christ, and when He is at the group's center, everything else will come together.

OU'RE INVITED!

TO GROW . . .

*To develop and reach maturity; thrive; to spring up;
come into existence from a source;*

WITH A GROUP . . .

*An assemblage of persons gathered or located together;
a number of individuals considered together because of similarities;*

TO EXPLORE . . .

*To investigate systematically; examine; search into or range over
for the purpose of discovery;*

NEW TOPICS

Subject of discussion or conversation.

MEETING

Date _____ Time _____

Place _____

_____

Contact _____

Phone _____

ONE

BUILDING RIGHT RELATIONSHIPS

How right are your relationships? Right relationships are essential not only in the family and in the church but also in the workplace. Many studies have shown that the primary reason people lose their job is because of poor relational skills. A friend of mine lost a great managerial position because she told another employee a bit of confidential news the boss had shared with her. Gossip destroys relationships in the family, church and neighborhood, as well as in the workplace.

I'm also reminded of a nursing-home resident who received indifferent service from the home's staff because she refused to stop barking instructions at them. I tried to help her understand the importance of good body language and a warm tone of voice. I failed. She continued to speak gruffly, and the staff continued giving their indifferent help. Love shows itself in our way of speaking.

One researcher claims that he can predict with 94 percent accuracy the failure or success of any marriage. His research uncovers a telling five to one ratio: "As long as there is five times as much positive feeling and interaction between husband and wife as there is negative, we found the marriage was likely to be stable."[1] The words we speak are all too often words of death instead of words of life (see Proverbs 18:21). The level of our love for others shows itself in the words we speak.

When someone has emotionally wounded us, we often disobey what Scripture says by talking to a third party instead of first talking with the person who hurt us (see Matthew 18:15). Just as unscriptural is our refusal to speak with the person we know to be hurting or upset by our behavior or words (see Matthew 5:23-24). Love means learning to listen non-defensively.

The goal of this lesson is to help you take an honest look at your relationships and how they line up with the truth of God's "love one another" commandments.

How would you define a right relationship? (Write out your answer before you read mine!)

_____

_____

_____

_____

To me, a right relationship is an open-armed approach to every person in my life, regardless of the way he or she treats me. In such a relationship, I feel no sense of separation, no unforgiven hurts, no underlying problems I refuse to discuss or choose to ignore. I am at peace with everyone as far as it depends on me (see Romans 12:18).

How did your definition of a right relationship differ from mine? What things would you change in your definition or my definition, and why would you make these changes?

_____

_____

_____

_____

A Closer Look at the Problem

Many of us look at a relationship rift and think first of the harm done to us. "I'm so mad at Jane. She was my maid of honor and she didn't even ask me to be in her wedding!" "I can't believe she didn't speak to me in the mall, when I know she saw me and looked right at me." "I feel totally unloved by my mother. She was selfish and self-centered. Mother left me with a babysitter while she ran off to fashion shows, spas, lunches with her girlfriends or bridge games. She never had time for me. How could anyone expect me to forgive her and give her a hug when I see her? I'd be a hypocrite."

The "poor me" approach is of course self-centered as opposed to God-centered. If we focus first on God's love for us that we can never deserve or earn, we may be more willing to respond with a God-inspired request such as, "Lord, I can't give love to this person. Please fill me with Your love and inspire me to do the loving thing."

Relationship problems end in separation when we refuse to work on changing our emotional responses to those who hurt us. It is virtually impossible to feel our way to new actions. If we wait until we feel loving before talking with the offending friend, the one who slighted us or the parent who gave us less love than we think we deserved, we will probably never respond. And the fire of love and friendship will be replaced with the smoldering ashes of bitterness.

Share a time when you were hurt by a family member, friend or coworker, and you let your negative feelings keep you from acting in love as commanded in God's Word. (Be sure you protect the identity of the person who injured you.)

_____

_____

_____

_____

Scripture reminds us that even the pagans love those who love them. Returning love for love is no big deal in Scripture. The challenge is to love those who hate you and use you (see Matthew 5:44).

A Closer Look at God's Truth

The Bible concerns itself with the words we speak, the negative thoughts we refuse to give up and the actions we take or refuse to take. Love is shown by words *and* actions.

Read Matthew 25:31-40; 1 John 3:10; and 1 John 4:12,19-21. Is Jesus commanding us to *feel* something or to *do* something in these Scriptures?

_____

_____

_____

_____

In answering this question, it is helpful to remember that the New Testament verb for "love" in these verses, *agapao*, is an action word. *Vine's Complete Expository Dictionary* explains, "Love can only be known from the actions it prompts. God's love is seen in the gift of His Son (1 John: 4:9,10). . . . Love had its perfect expression among men in the Lord Jesus Christ."[2]

The Bible also uses the word *phileo* for "love." This is the *feeling* word for "love," best translated as "tender affections." *Phileo* is used of God's love for His Son and of God's love for us. But please note: "*Phileo* is never used in a command to men to love God."[3]

After reading the above Scriptures, we can see clearly that the way we treat the least significant or most obnoxious persons in our lives is a barometer of our love for Jesus Christ. Since love is known by the actions it takes, let's look at some of the Bible's "love one another" commandments to learn how our heavenly Father expects us to act.

Look up the following references and write the key action word (such as "serve" or "forgive") for each passage.

Romans 12:10 _____ to one another.
Romans 12:13 _____ with God's people.
Romans 12:14 _____ and do not _____.
Romans 15:1 _____ the failings of the weak.
2 Corinthians 13:12 _____ each other.
Galatians 5:13 _____ one another.
Ephesians 5:21 _____ to one another.
Colossians 3:13 _____ with each other and

_____.

1 Thessalonians 5:11 _____ one another and
_____ each other.
James 5:16 _____ for each other.

What are some of the reasons you find it easy or difficult to maintain right relationships? Write down the names of specific people in your life as you answer.

With friends

_____
_____
_____

With family members

_____
_____
_____

In the workplace

_____

_____

_____

In church

_____

_____

_____

Sometimes when I read the "love one another" passages, I experience spiritual claustrophobia, a sense of too much togetherness. I prefer not to confess my sins to anyone but God. I'm not too keen on hugging, much less greeting with a kiss. I prefer hugging myself to greeting others with sisterly affection. Daily I would feel smothered by a gigantic blanket of guilt if I had to first feel like doing these things. But when I live in step with God, I am obedient to these "love one another" Scriptures, even when I feel negative about the required actions. Constantly I must remind myself: *Love is an action I take, not a sentiment I feel.*

A Closer Look at My Own Heart

Scripture tells us that the heart is deceitful above all else (see Jeremiah 17:9). This is why, with prayer, we need to evaluate and discover how right our relationships are.

RATING YOUR RELATIONSHIPS

The following test is designed to help you rate yourself in the area of relationships. Beside each of the listed behaviors, place the number that best describes how often you engage in the behavior:

1—Almost always	4—Occasionally
2—With few exceptions	5—Rarely
3—Usually	6—Never

____ 1. I make myself move toward a person who has hurt me, as opposed to withdrawing. This means that I reach out with an act of kindness to the person, I talk to the person at a social event, I telephone the person, and so forth (see Romans 12:17).

____ 2. I forgive people when they hurt me, even if they do not admit their wrongs or ask to be forgiven (see Colossians 3:13).

____ 3. I go to other people as soon as I realize I have hurt or upset them and ask to be forgiven (see Matthew 5:23-24).

____ 4. I attribute good motives to people when they hurt me ("I'm sure they meant me no harm"), as opposed to deciding someone has deliberately hurt me (see 1 Corinthians 13:6-7).

____ 5. I receive criticism without attacking the person criticizing me and/or without defending myself (see Matthew 5:11).

____ 6. I share what is good and helpful for building others up, as opposed to gossip and giving a bad report (see Ephesians 4:29).

____ 7. I make my mind dwell on things that are true, pure and excellent, as opposed to dwelling on the wrongs done to me (see Philippians 4:8).

____ 8. I am quick to listen and slow to speak (see James 1:19).

____ 9. I am careful not to judge anyone (see Matthew 7:1).

____10. I practice hospitality without grumbling (see 1 Peter 4:9).

____ 11. I consider others more important than myself and am happy to let another car move in front of me or to give up my plans for the day in order to serve another (see Philippians 2:3).

____ 12. I give comfort to those hurting—as opposed to butting into the conversation with my problems, criticizing the speaker for his or her feelings, or making light of the other person's problems (see Romans 12:15).

____ 13. I confess my faults to at least one other Christian (see James 5:16).

____ 14. I receive all people warmly and affectionately, even if they are poor, needy, repetitious, in need of a bath, boring or obnoxious (see Romans 15:7; James 2:1).

____ 15. I speak words of encouragement to others, as opposed to pointing out their faults (see Hebrews 3:13; 10:25).

GRADING YOURSELF

If the majority of the numbers you wrote are 1s, 2s and 3s, you have good relationships. A majority of numbers 4 to 6 indicates behavior that is less than God's best for you.

In what area(s) do you most need to grow in obedience to God's relationship commandments?

_____
_____
_____
_____

Share this with one other person, and pray for one another.

Action Steps I Can Take Today

Put your new attitudes into action. Choose the most troubling relationship in your life at this time. Prayerfully ask God to show you where you have failed to love this person God's way. Confess your sin.

Next, ask God to tell you the best way for you to express His love to this difficult family member, friend or acquaintance. Wait upon the Lord and listen. When you think you have heard from God, act immediately! Place the phone call, write the note, stop by with flowers—whatever action the Holy Spirit inspires.

Notes

1. John Gottman, *Why Marriages Succeed or Fail* (New York: Simon & Schuster, 1994), p. 57.
2. W. E. Vine, *Vine's Complete Expository Dictionary* (Nashville, TN: Thomas Nelson Inc., 1984), pp. 381-382.
3. Ibid., p. 382.

ℒOVING OUR NEIGHBORS

I recently read a story in my hometown newspaper about a distraught man who entered the emergency room of a local hospital and announced that he planned to kill himself. A savvy secretary asked the man if he loved himself. When the man said no, the secretary replied, "If you are here, asking for help, it seems to me that you do love yourself."

Whenever I teach this lesson about loving our neighbors, I know I will be asked one question: "Don't I have to learn to love myself before you expect me to love others?" My reply is always the same: "No, the problem is that you already love yourself too much."

Why would I reply so harshly when I usually don't know anything about the questioner? First of all, my answer lines up with the Bible. Second, nowhere in Scripture are we commanded to love ourselves. Scripture assumes we love ourselves. The goal of this chapter is to help you understand the biblical truth about loving others as much as we love ourselves.

A Closer Look at the Problem

The Matthew 22:39 command to love others as much as we love ourselves uses the familiar Greek verb for "love," *agapao*, which we defined in chapter 1 as an action verb. To love someone is to look out for, to take care of, or to prefer him or her. We may not feel good about ourselves on any one day of the week, but the vast majority of us will take care of our own needs before those of another.

Listed below are some ways we may show that we love ourselves more than we love our neighbors. Remember, to love another person means to treat him or her as well as we treat ourselves. Read each of the seven questions and its accompanying action examples, and then determine which question is the most difficult for you to answer affirmatively.

1. *Do you excuse your neighbor's behavior as graciously as you excuse your own?* When you arrive late for church, you bless your tardiness

with the excuse that the phone rang at the last minute or that you're overworked and needed a few more winks of sleep. If a neighbor shows up late for church, you might label her inconsiderate and disruptive as she climbs over you to get to her seat, never stopping to think that her reason for being late may be better than yours. When you say unkind words to your spouse or children, you excuse yourself because of your exhaustion or your difficult day. If your neighbor says unkind words, you label him judgmental and mean-spirited.

2. *Do you accept your neighbor's emotions as easily as you accept your own?* When you're depressed, it's because your family situation is difficult, the dog died or your mother is ill. If your neighbor gets depressed, you accuse him or her of self-pity. Your anger is usually justified; your neighbor's anger reveals his or her immaturity.

3. *Do you guard your neighbor's good reputation as carefully as you guard your own?* You don't gossip about yourself. However, you may not hesitate to tell your friends about the lazy mother who sleeps in and lets her children fix breakfast, a coworker who chats on the phone with friends during work hours, or a friend who often forgets luncheon engagements or your birthday celebration.

4. *Do you take actions to ensure that your neighbor is as well fed, clothed and housed as your own family?* If your neighbor is unemployed and without benefits, do you share your paycheck, so the family may pay their bills and buy groceries and clothing with the same ease with which you pay for yours? Would you be willing to cancel your Colorado ski trip in order to bless a missionary friend with desperately needed funds?

5. *Do you try to anticipate and meet your neighbor's unspoken needs in the same way you want yours to be anticipated and met?* If your neighbor is painting or wallpapering, do you offer to help? If your neighbor is moving, do you offer to help him or her pack the truck or serve him or her breakfast on the day of the move without being asked?

6. *Do you give up your planned activity to join in the activity desired by your closest neighbor?* Your closest neighbor may be your spouse, your child, a friend or a relative. If you can't possibly think about missing the home and garden show, but your spouse wants you to attend the ball game, which activity would you choose?

7. *Do you forgive your neighbor as readily as you forgive yourself?* If you dent the front fender of your car, you probably won't hold a grudge against yourself. But if your neighbor borrows your car and dents the fender, you might mentally or verbally accuse them of driving carelessly or too fast.

Which question is the most difficult for you to answer affirmatively? Why do you think this is so?

_____
_____
_____
_____
_____

Name some other ways we fail to treat others as graciously, kindly or generously as we treat ourselves.

_____
_____
_____
_____
_____
_____

A Closer Look at God's Truth

When Jesus was asked which was the greatest commandment, He replied, " 'Love the Lord your God with all your heart and with all your soul and with all your mind.' This is the first and greatest commandment. And the second is like it: 'Love your neighbor as yourself' " (Matthew 22:37-39). According to Jesus, how many commandments are there in this quote? Two, of course. But if you count loving yourself as a commandment, you end up with three commandments.

In Ephesians 5:28-29, Paul writes, "In this same way [as Christ loved the church], husbands ought to love their wives as their own bodies. He who loves his wife loves himself. After all, no one ever hated his own body, but he feeds and cares for it, just as Christ does the church." Does God's Word assume that men love their bodies or that men need to be trained to love their bodies?

_____

_____

_____

_____

Scripture maintains that Christian love is best demonstrated in our actions, not our words. Read Matthew 25:31-40. The goats in this passage seem puzzled by their separation from the sheep. What kind of churchgoers do the goats represent?

_____

_____

_____

_____

What does 1 John 3:14-15 say about the seriousness of our relationships with one another? How do you feel as you read this Scripture?

_____

_____

_____

_____

Read 1 John 3:16-18. What is the one sure way we know that God loves us?

_____

_____

_____

_____

Write a definition of love that includes biblical truth on this subject.

_____

_____

_____

_____

The following passage from *Vine's Complete Expository Dictionary* provides a more complete definition of biblical love than we read in chapter 1:

> Love can be known only from the action it prompts. God's love is . . . an exercise of the Divine will, in deliberate choice, made without assignable cause. . . . Christian love . . . is not an impulse from the feelings, it does not always run with the natural inclinations, nor does it spend itself only upon those from whom some affinity is discovered. . . . Love seeks opportunity to do good to all men.[1]

A Closer Look at My Own Heart

Read Luke 9:23-24. What does it mean to you to take up your cross daily?

_____

_____

_____

_____

Write a definition of self-denial.

_____

_____

_____

_____

_____

Circle the letters of each of the following ways you have difficulty in denying yourself:

a. *Self-importance*—If you walk into a gathering of people wondering who will speak to you, who will notice you, who will remember your birthday or prayer request, you are choosing self-importance. Since Christ calls you to deny self-importance, you need to welcome the lonely, befriend the friendless, listen to the ignored, hug the hurting and pray for the despondent.

b. *Self-occupation*—If you arrive at a meeting or church gathering with your lists of people to see and things to do, you may be so self-occupied that you ignore the hurting people around you or fail to hear the person telling you that she will have surgery the next day. To deny self-occupation is to remember to say, "Hi, how are you doing?" before you blurt out a question such as, "Can you possibly help me with Bible School next week?" Too often we only agree to help people when we are free to choose the time, the place and the way. Unfortunately, people need help when we have made previous plans. Denying self-occupation means letting your wallpapering or yard work wait until after you cook a meal for a sick neighbor or mow an elderly person's lawn.

c. *Self-affection*—If you overtalk about your vacation, achievements or family members at the expense of another's need to talk, you are allowing self-affection to ruin your listening skills. How well do you listen? Do you listen so that you may find a time to turn the conversation back on yourself, or do you listen to understand what the other person is saying?

d. *Self-protection*—If your ego wants to defend itself against criticism and correction, you are putting self-protection in the forefront. When you are in the self-protective mode, you criticize the person who dared to criticize you: "The way she treats her husband—how dare she tell me I've wronged mine." Or, if you don't directly criticize the person, you raise yourself above the one criticizing you: "I certainly won't listen to anything spoken that harshly and without love."

e. *Self-inspection*—If you check your feelings to see if you should attend church, read the Bible or say yes to sex with our spouse, you are letting your feelings override God's instructions. How much wiser it is to check your decisions or commitments. God calls you to live in obedience to His Word and His Spirit; He does not call you to obey your emotions.

f. *Self-sufficiency*—God has decreed an interdependent lifestyle for believers. We are members of one another (see 1 Corinthians 12:27). Is it difficult for you to allow another person to change a tire on your car when you have a backache, or to clean your house, rake your lawn or care for your children when you are ill? If you find it difficult to ask for help or if you refuse offered help when you need to receive it, you are separating and isolating yourself from the Body of Christ. To deny self-sufficiency is to admit that you need help and will receive it when offered.

What examples can you add to this self-denial list?

_____

_____

_____

_____

Read John 13:34-35 and Romans 13:8-10. List the reasons for loving your neighbors as you love yourself.

_____

_____

_____

_____

Action Steps I Can Take Today

What one thing can you start to do today to stimulate your growth in self-denial? (For example, is there an offer of help that you need to accept?)

_____

_____

_____

_____

What will you do with God's help to grow in self-denial this week?

_____

_____

_____

_____

Note
1. W. E. Vine, *Vine's Complete Expository Dictionary* (Nashville, TN: Thomas Nelson Inc., 1984), pp. 381-382.

THREE

HONORING ONE ANOTHER

I can still remember the office where the professional counselor and I sat. There was a restrained stillness before she spoke her question. "Bobbie," she asked as she leaned forward to touch my hand, "do you by chance have an exaggerated sense of self-importance?"

Ouch! I knew my counselor would not have asked unless she felt I suffered from a bloated sense of self-importance. I didn't answer. Instead, I took the question home with me. After days of self-pity and denial, I finally accepted the question as legitimate. I decided to spend time in prayer to receive the Holy Spirit's illumination of any truth behind this probing question. In His time, God showed me my incessant need to speak in every committee meeting and every Bible study I attended; how I blocked every driver who dared to try to cut in on me; my impatience in listening to others speak, causing me to interrupt so I could talk; my expecting my opinions to be accepted as "the truth"; my tendency to elevate myself by announcing to others my good deeds that God wants me to forget, send on to heaven and wait for His reward.

Acknowledging failures isn't fun, but the first step toward change is realizing where we are failing. When the scales of blindness fall off, we see ourselves as others do. That's exhilarating! This Bible study provides a time to stretch our faith and acknowledge our failures. As you study how to honor one another, remember that the Lord compassionately corrects while the enemy fiercely condemns.

A Closer Look at the Problem

I appreciate some of the strong synonyms listed for the word "honor" in *Roget's Thesaurus*: "acclaim, admire, appreciate, compliment, lionize, look up to." I remember a time when I felt blessed in all these ways by a reception given in my honor by a Bible study group I had taught for 13 years.

The women honored me with a scrapbook of more than a hundred letters of appreciation. The Bible Study Core Group took the time to uncover funny incidents in my life and presented a "This Is Your Life, Bobbie" skit. There was a corsage, decorations, poems, tears and laughter. But what I appreciated most was the fact that each woman had interrupted her busy schedule to attend the reception and write a loving letter in appreciation of me. I truly felt lionized.

Think of a special time in your life when you felt honored. What made the event so special to you? Recall all the emotions you felt at this time and why you felt them.

_____

_____

_____

_____

Describe a time when you honored a friend or family member.

_____

_____

_____

_____

A Closer Look at God's Truth

In chapter 2 we looked at the *actions* of love. Today we focus our attention on the *attitude* of love. This lesson will place a magnifying glass over the commandment found in Romans 12:10: "Outdo one another in showing honor" (*RSV*) or "in honor let each set his neighbor above himself."[1]

THE ATTITUDE OF LOVE

The Godhead is our role model for considering others more important than ourselves. Read John 14:13; 15:26 and 17:24 and record how the members of the Godhead glorify each other.

_____

_____

_____

_____

When you are part of a group, what are some things you do to call attention to yourself?

_____

_____

_____

_____

What are some specific things you might do to call attention to others, as the members of the Godhead do for one another?

_____

_____

_____

_____

Read Romans 12:10. Whom should you honor? The word "honor" in your Bible translation might be "value," "esteem," "respect" or some other word.

_____

_____

_____

_____

In most translations of the Bible, you will find the noun form of the Greek word for "honor" translated "price." We know the great value God places on us when we realize the enormity of the price He paid to make us His own:

> For God has bought you with a great price. So use every part of your body to give glory back to God, because he owns it (1 Corinthians 6:20, *TLB*).

In 1 Peter 2:17 we are told to honor everyone, which would include the poor and the rich; the common person and the king; the ignorant and the educated; people without positions and people with positions; dirty, smelly people and clean, neat, perfumed people.

In the world's view, what things make a person worthy of honor?

_____

_____

_____

Read Genesis 1:26-27 and Psalm 8:3-9 and compare the world's reasons for honoring others with God's reasons for honoring all people.

_____

_____

_____

_____

We honor all women and men because we are original, one-of-a-kind masterpieces, created by the master artist of the universe in His image. When we honor others, we are honoring their Creator. When we dishonor others, we dishonor God.

SPECIFIC PEOPLE TO HONOR
Read the following Scriptures. Beside each listed Scripture, identify the persons we are told to honor.

Philippians 2:25,29-30 _____

1 Timothy 5:3 _____

1 Timothy 5:17 _____

1 Timothy 6:1-2 _____

1 Peter 2:17 _____

1 Peter 3:1,7 _____

In what ways was this list of honored men and women unusual for first-century society and even for today?

_____

_____

_____

_____

What a fresh word of hope these Scriptures must have brought to first-century wives, widows and common people—the *least* members of society. Today, this would be the same as telling us to honor homeless people. Notice that the passage in 1 Peter 2 lists all people as worthy of honor before it singles out the king. The Christian faith is revolutionary in commanding us to honor the least significant members of society because of their intrinsic worth as people created by God.

SPECIFIC WAYS TO SHOW HONOR

Beside each of the following Scriptures, write specific ways we are told to honor others.

Leviticus 19:32 _____

Romans 16:16 _____

1 Corinthians 11:33 _____

1 Peter 4:9 _____

1 Peter 5:5 _____

One way we honor one another is by being polite and showing courtesy toward one another. Unfortunately, there has been a noticeable decrease in civility and an increase in rudeness in our society.

Name some of the manners most parents used to teach their children that few parents teach children today.

_____
_____
_____
_____

Men and children no longer stand when a woman enters the room. Doors are no longer held open for women or the elderly. Some women even scorn the common courtesies that men traditionally performed, leaving males bewildered about what today's women want. Recently I sat on the floor of a Sunday School class while none of the men present offered this 67-year-old woman a chair. Children are no longer taught to respect their elders. How many families wait and have blessing before anyone starts to eat? How often is the gift of hospitality exercised in Christian homes today? Although these examples may seem trivial or superficial today, these behaviors are outward signs of a wide-ranging breakdown of respect and increase of selfishness.

Specific Ways to Show Respect

Our body language and tone of voice quickly communicate to another person our respect or disrespect. A teenage girl once confided to me, "Everyone I try to talk to at our church coffee hour keeps looking over my shoulder to see who they can talk to next." This young woman felt deeply rejected by church members and later attempted suicide.

Scripture assumes we like to talk. It never encourages us to talk more, but instead in Proverbs 18:13 we are told it is shameful behavior to speak before listening. James 1:19 commands us to listen before speaking. All too often we listen to speak instead of listening for understanding. We listen with our answers running in our heads, waiting to add our two-cents worth to the conversation.

When we listen without interrupting, when we stay focused on the subject the speaker has introduced instead of turning the conversation on ourselves and what we want to talk about, we honor the other person. You may be amazed at how difficult it is to learn to listen to understand, instead of listening for the moment when you can interrupt and speak. That's because listening for understanding requires death to self. If you want to have your heart's number-one interest revealed, take the Three Q Test.

A Closer Look at My Own Heart

The Three Q Test

Our ability to listen, or our lack of that ability, quickly reveals the focus of our hearts. Are we more self-centered than others-centered? A salesman once shared with me his secret of success: "I always ask three questions of my customers before I speak about myself or one of my products." He finds something in the customer's office that indicates a hobby or interest. He then expresses his interest in the customer by asking at least three questions about the customer's family or interests.

The average person, untrained in listening skills, rarely if ever asks three questions about any subject someone *else* introduces. If it's a conversation about a bright child or darling grandchild, the average listener will ask one question and then say, "You know my granddaughter called me last night to tell me she loved me." If the topic is surgery, again we are good for one or two questions before we say something like, "My father underwent that same surgery last year!" If the talk centers on favorite vacation spots, one question is normal before the listener says, "I was in Hawaii last year! We loved it!"

It's not that we should never talk about our families and our activities; it's just that one of the best ways to honor someone is to show a genuine interest in what he or she is saying. Try asking someone at least three questions before you say "I" or "we." Here's an example of a listener who honored the speaker with three questions.

> *Speaker:* "I'm speechless with joy! Our first granddaughter was born last week! And she's such a sweetheart."
>
> *Listener, asking question one:* "Wonderful! Tell me all about her. Do you have a picture?"
>
> *Speaker:* "You know I do! Let me show you Grandma's Brag Book."
>
> *Listener, looking at picture and asking question two:* "Such a beautiful baby! Who does she look like?"
>
> *Speaker:* "My daughter. We compared baby pictures, and she's identical to her mother."
>
> *Listener, asking question three:* "Were you there when she was born? I forget where your daughter lives."
>
> *Speaker:* "Sue is just 50 miles away. I stayed with her for ten days. We'll be seeing baby Courtney once a week when possible. I just love her."

The Three Q Test is one you learn to pass by intentionally asking three questions before you speak. If you spend a day just listening to others at the fitness club, the office, the beauty parlor and/or the church, you'll discover how seldom people honor one another through listening.

RESPECTFUL RESPONSES

Our responses also reveal disrespect for others, usually in one of four ways:

> 1. *We reject another's feelings and tell the speaker that he or she has no right to feel the way he or she does.*
>
> > *Speaker:* "I feel like I'm a burden to the world, lying in this bed, helpless and paralyzed."

Disrespectful Response: "How can you say such a thing? You know you're a blessing to everyone who visits you."

Respectful Response: "It must be really tough having to ask everyone to do for you when you'd like to be doing for yourself."

2. *We challenge the speaker's perception of a controversial issue.*

Speaker: "Vitamins are the best cure to date found for cancer."

Disrespectful Response: "That's hocus-pocus and the most stupid thing I've ever heard."

Respectful Response: "How interesting! Tell me how you came to place so much trust in vitamins."

3. *We give cliché answers to a speaker's problem.*

Speaker: "I'm so worried my son might experiment with sex now that he's in high school."

Disrespectful Response: "It's obvious you're not trusting God."

Respectful Response: "That must be a big concern for you."

4. *We fail to use the Three Q Test.*

Speaker: "My son just made starting quarterback on his high school team."

Disrespectful Response: "That's nice. My son just made the honor society."

Respectful Response: "I'm sure you're proud of him. How long has he played football? Is he a junior or senior this year? Does he plan to go on with his football career in college?"

Write down the ways you would welcome Jesus if He dropped by during your Bible study.

_____

_____

_____

_____

_____

Can we do less for anyone God places in our lives? Remember, whenever we honor the least of society, we honor Jesus Christ our Lord (see Matthew 25:35-40).

Action Steps I Can Take Today

Ask yourself, *Do I honor people because of their position, wealth and knowledge or because they are divine originals, created by the Lord of the universe? Do I listen with my answers running in my head or do I listen to understand?*

Practice respectful answers by writing down how you would respond to the remarks below. (Remember to show respect for the speaker by responding to what is true in what he or she says. Refer to the examples in this chapter, if you need help.)

1. *Speaker:* "I feel like a real nut for forgetting my lines in the church play. I'm so embarrassed."

   Respectful Answer:

   _____
   _____
   _____
   _____

2. *Speaker:* "I believe the Bible is a book of fairy tales."

   Respectful Answer:

   _____
   _____
   _____
   _____

3. *Speaker:* "I know I'm going to get the flu that's going around."

   Respectful Answer:

   _____
   _____
   _____
   _____

4. *Speaker:* "I got an A+ on my math test!"

Respectful Answer:

_____

_____

_____

_____

_____

To see how well you did, check your answers with the following possible responses. Your answers probably won't be exactly the same as those below, but they should be in the same spirit.

1. *Respectful Answer:* "It must have been hard for you to stick in there when you felt like running off the stage and never returning." (Disrespect would challenge the speaker's emotions: "Well, that's the silliest thing I ever heard. It was only a church play.")

2. *Respectful Answer:* "I'd be interested to know more about your biblical studies that led you to that conclusion. Did you study alone or did you go to Bible school?" (Disrespect would put down the speaker's conclusions: "If you'd really studied the Bible, you wouldn't say such a thing.")

3. *Respectful Answer:* "This year's flu seems to be of a more serious variety. Have you been exposed to it?" (Disrespect would trivialize the speaker's worry and also give a cliché answer: "Why would you say such a thing like that? What we fear always comes upon us.")

4. *Respectful Answer:* "That's wonderful. Which math class are you taking? Who is your teacher? How much studying did you have to do? You must feel good doing so well after all your hard work." (Disrespect would turn the conversation back on self: "That's nice. Math was my most difficult subject, but I managed to make straight As.")

To whom do you need to show honor? What one thing could you do this week to show honor to that person?

_____
_____
_____
_____

How will you put these new listening skills into practice this week?

_____
_____
_____
_____

Note

1. W.J. Conybeare, *The Life and Epistles of Paul* (Grand Rapids, MI: Wm. B. Eerdmans Publishing Company, 1949).

FOUR

Encouraging One Another

I remember little from my childhood, but one event stands chiseled in my memory. When I was eight years old, God miraculously healed me from a kidney disease that the doctors had said would probably be fatal. After nine months of bed rest, I returned to church, stepping out of the car wobbly on my toothpick legs. Many members of our small church rushed up to give me a warm but general greeting such as, "Oh, it's so good to have you back." But Mrs. Meadows, a missionary friend, took my hand in hers, stooped down to look me directly in my eyes and said, "Bobbie Lee, God saved you for a very special purpose." My life was touched by God through Mrs. Meadows. She encouraged me in the Lord.

We have studied the *actions* of love (chapter 2) and *attitude* of love (chapter 3). In this chapter we examine the *words* of love. We'll discover fresh, new ways to encourage those whose lives touch ours, and we'll appreciate together our God, the God of *all* encouragement.

A Closer Look at the Problem

A Checkup of Our Daily Speech

Psychologists estimate that each day we have about 700 opportunities to speak. Talkative people utter about 12,000 sentences a day, which works out to approximately 100,000 words. How many of those words are encouraging? How many are discouraging? God's Word clearly instructs us to encourage one another daily (see Hebrews 3:13) and speak only words that build up others (see Ephesians 4:29), for we will be held responsible for every careless word we speak (see Matthew 12:36-37).

Are most of your words positive or negative?

> I estimate that ___ percent of my words are negative and discouraging and that ___ percent of my words are encouraging to others.

THE ENEMY OF ENCOURAGEMENT

Before we learn some of the many ways to encourage one another, let's look at the enemy of encouragement. The enemy is *criticism*, the discourager. We need to remind ourselves that criticism changes no one and often becomes counterproductive. (If it worked, think how nice we'd all be!) Criticism ranks highest in the arsenal of people weapons.

I believe we must avoid a backward look at poor behavior and instead focus on what we'd like to see happen.

Poor: "How many times do I have to tell you to wipe your shoes on the mat before coming in the house?"

Good: "Stephen, please go back and wipe your feet on the mat."

Poor: "Why do I have to tell you a hundred times that the washing machine's leaking? Can't you ever put my needs on the top of your to-do list?"

Good: "Honey, the washing machine is leaking so much I'm afraid it might ruin our floor. I'd really appreciate your coming to see what you can do as soon as this last load finishes spinning."

Poor: "I'd appreciate one decent dinner a week. Can't you ever come up with something better than TV dinners?"

Good: "Honey, do you think we could have one of your delicious cooked dinners tonight? I'll clean up if you'll cook."

THE POWER OF OUR WORDS

The Bible tells us that the power of life and death is in our words (see Proverbs 18:21). When discouraged by criticism, I overeat and hold a pity party to which I invite no one but myself. A dangerous downward spiral of negative thinking begins with my telling myself, *I never do anything right. I'm ineffective in the kingdom of God, and no one likes me.* Too often I allow one perceived failure or one critical remark to trigger depression.

I used to neglect filing my fingernails until one day a friend noticed that I had filed them. She took my hands in her lovely manicured ones and exclaimed, "Bobbie, you fixed your fingernails! How nice they look!" Ever since (with an occasional slip), I have filed my nails.

We can help create change in every life that touches ours by looking for something to praise and then speaking it out daily. *But one word of caution:* Just as we want to criticize actions and not people, we want to praise actions and not people. If you say, "You are the nicest person in the world!" the recipient of the praise may mentally refuse the exaggerated compliment, thinking instead of all the people nicer than he or she. How much better to say, "I appreciate your warm greeting and friendly smile."

Poor: "You are the most faithful Christian I know."

Good: "I appreciate your faithfulness in teaching the Bible all these years."

REASONS FOR CRITICISM

Although there are many explanations for why we criticize, there are four main reasons why we misuse words this way:

1. Our parents may have earned graduate degrees in negativity while raising us.

2. The newspapers, Internet and TV daily drench our minds with global accounts of diabolic events.

3. We may subconsciously criticize others as a way of building up ourselves. When we say something like, "Sally never makes a home-cooked meal for her husband, Jerry," we imply that we always do our own cooking and take better care of our husband.

4. We don't want to give anything up. To encourage others costs us something. In order to build them up, we have to set self aside.

Regardless of how little we know about encouragement and/or how few role models we find, we can learn to "encourage one another daily, as long as it is called Today" (Hebrews 3:13).

A Closer Look at God's Truth

If you look up the words "comfort," "exhort" and "encourage" in a New Testament concordance or a Greek dictionary of the New Testament, you will discover that there is only one Greek verb for all three translations. The word is *parakaleo*, which means "a calling to one's side." The Holy

Spirit is called the *parakletos* because He is the one who comes beside us to help, comfort and encourage us.

Read the following Scriptures in as many Bible translations as possible and list the different verbs used to capture the richness of the verb "to call to one's side."

John 11:19

_____
_____
_____
_____

1 Timothy 5:1

_____
_____
_____
_____

Hebrews 3:13

_____
_____
_____
_____

In the following Scriptures we find the noun *paraklesis,* "the one who comes to help." Read the following passages in as many Bible translations as possible and list the different words used for an encourager.

John 14:16

_____
_____
_____

Acts 4:36

_____
_____
_____

2 Corinthians 1:3

_____

_____

_____

_____

Based on these Scriptures, what do you think the Bible means when it tells us to encourage one another daily?

_____

_____

_____

_____

Encouragement can be conveyed by our physical presence, by our practical help or in our spoken and written words. An encourager comforts, consoles, exhorts, takes another's side and helps. We can read the Bible from Genesis to Revelation with joy in our hearts because God is the God of all encouragement.

Read Genesis 3:14-15,21 and Revelation 21:1-4. In what ways do these Scriptures comfort you?

_____

_____

_____

_____

List at least two other Scriptures that encourage you. (If you have trouble thinking of two passages, read Romans 8:31 and Philippians 1:6.)

_____

_____

_____

_____

How God views His children excites, exhilarates and encourages. Scriptures reveal that our heavenly Father sees us complete in Christ: We are holy, blameless and glorified saints. God speaks of us today as we will one day be. He knows the power of words (see Romans 8:30; 2 Corinthians 3:18; Colossians 1:2,22 and 1 Peter 2:9-10).

Read Hebrews 3:12-13. Why is it crucial to encourage others daily?

_____
_____
_____
_____
_____

We think that we have to point out others' faults to keep them from sinning, but Scripture tells us we keep others from sinning by encouraging them. Note that it is not clear in this passage who benefits from the encouragement: the speaker or the listener. I believe that it is both.

A Closer Look at My Own Heart

Matthew 12:34 reminds us that "out of the overflow of the heart the mouth speaks." Our words are a belated announcement to the world of what we have been thinking and feeling.

Read Ephesians 4:29. Place the stethoscope of this verse to your heart and ask God to reveal any negative patterns of unwholesome speech that you might have, such as gossip, anger, put-downs or joking at the expense of others. Write down those times.

_____
_____
_____
_____

Ask God to also reveal times when you have failed to encourage others. Write down those times.

_____
_____
_____
_____

Action Steps I Can Take Today

Here are some ways to encourage others. Circle the letter of one or two of the following ideas you are challenged to try this week:

a. Pray for others and let them know that you are remembering them. We all are encouraged when people remember our prayer requests and tell us, "You asked me to pray for your father last week. How is he doing?"

b. Tell your children and grandchildren how special they are to the Lord. I read of one mother who whispered into each child's ear as she tucked them in bed, "I know God has a special plan for your life."

c. Speak your positive thoughts to the person who inspired them. Don't just *think* that the speaker is excellent, the choir inspirational, the ushers warm and friendly. Go beyond just thinking that your granddaughter looks great in red or that you're proud of your son's achievements as a Christian, a student, a professional or a father. To encourage more, become aware of your positive thoughts and *verbalize* them—daily!

d. Recognize others' God-given gifts. Say, "I appreciate what you said in the meeting. It made sense," or "I appreciate the way you get here early to set up the chairs," or "I appreciate your ministry to my children in Sunday School."

e. Stop criticizing others. Try what the late Catherine Marshall did. One day the Lord brought to her mind Romans 14:13: "So let us stop criticizing one another" (*Moffatt*). Her assignment that day was not to speak one negative word all day long. She found it difficult and so will the majority of Christians.

f. Encourage others with notes or phone calls. When people feel down and discover a note of encouragement in the mail, they are uplifted.

g. Spur others on by offering a helping hand when they want to quit. One night when I returned home from an exhausting speaking schedule to get ready for weekend guests, I discovered piles of neat, clean, laundered linens that I needed to be prepared for my guests—a love gift from my upstairs neighbor. Strengthened, I felt I could make it through the weekend.

h. In a group setting, practice encouraging others on their birthday, anniversary or any other special days. Every group member tells the "special day" person one thing they appreciate about him or her. The honored person ends up feeling warm and loved.

i. Institute a "Family Night" in your household—a night of encouraging one member. All other family members tell the one person being affirmed one thing they appreciate about him or her. Choose a different family member to encourage the next week.

Which way did you circle? Write down specifically how you will put this step into action this week.

_____
_____
_____
_____

Pray daily, using this prayer or one of your own:

Dear Father,
You are the God of all encouragement and You live in me. I confess that I am quick to criticize and slow to encourage others. I ask Your forgiveness. May this be a day of bright beginnings for me as I decide to be the encourager You have equipped me to be through Your indwelling Holy Spirit. In Jesus' name, amen.

FIVE

HANDLING CONFRONTATION

If you have a problem with another person, how are you most likely to handle it? Do you confront the person, avoid the person, talk about the person to a third party, or do you forgive and work toward forgetting?

In this chapter, we will learn when to rebuke and when to remain quiet about another's thoughtlessness, ineffectiveness in a job, or sin. We'll also consider how to talk over your problem with the one who hurt you. As we speak about confrontation, we need to remember that in Scripture we are called to put away criticism, malice, revenge and hurtful words. We are called to put on compassion, kindness, humility, gentleness, patience and love—even when rebuking or admonishing another person.

A Closer Look at the Problem

HOW GOSSIP HURTS
When we avoid confrontation, our first reaction is usually to gossip. The following true story of church gossip illustrates the pain, ineffectiveness and damage caused by gossip.

Many people in Grace Church disliked the way Miss Smith, the choir director, led the time of informal, contemporary worship. A trained musician, she waved her arms excessively and chatted away between choruses, distracting some congregants from centering on the Lord. And she treated the congregation as a choir instead of people who had gathered to worship.

No one spoke to Miss Smith about the problem. Members complained among themselves and some spoke with the pastor, letting him know that Miss Smith was not their favorite worship leader. The pastor, a nonconfronter, chose to ignore the congregational rumblings against her.

Problems intensified when a new assistant pastor, an experienced song leader, joined the church staff. The senior pastor asked him to lead the informal service of congregational worship without first speaking to Miss Smith. The assistant pastor excitedly agreed, ignorant of the minefield waiting to explode around him. Minutes before Miss Smith entered the sanctuary with the choir the next Sunday, the senior pastor whispered in her ear that the new assistant pastor would replace her as worship leader, starting that day.

She was bewildered, hurt and angry. After worship, she confronted the assistant pastor and accused him of stealing her job. An angry encounter followed, both spoke harshly, and then they avoided one another.

Finally, the new assistant pastor asked the senior pastor for a full explanation of Miss Smith's anger. After listening to the story, the assistant explained his awkward position. Shortly afterwards, he invited Miss Smith to share her feelings and perspective with him. In listening to her, the assistant pastor realized that she felt deserted and hurt by her friends' lack of support of her as worship leader. The assistant explained to her that she was a popular choir director but not as popular as a worship leader.

Miss Smith was understandably hurt and disappointed, wishing she had received constructive criticism and an opportunity to change her style of worship leadership, but she was also relieved. Now she understood why her friends seemed distant and unsupportive. The truth hurt, but it also set her free. Healing and restoration happened between the assistant pastor and Miss Smith and between her and her friends.

If you had been a church member who disliked Miss Smith's style of worship leadership, would you have spoken to Miss Smith, gossiped about the problem with other church members, or gone to the pastor? Explain your answer.

_____

_____

_____

_____

Why We Gossip

Gather together two or three people and it won't be long before someone disappoints, angers, hurts or frustrates someone else. We talk to others about people who have displeased us. We gossip. Gossip, in turn, sows seeds of distrust and gives us negative attitudes toward those whom Christ has called us to love.

Our overarching problem is an inability to handle confrontation. We avoid talking with the one we have displeased or the one who has displeased us. If we refuse to talk about a problem with the person(s) involved, we most often end up gossiping. Gossip is the number one relationship problem in many churches, offices, factories, neighborhoods—everywhere.

My family and I lived for 13 years in a neighborhood shared with four to eight Christian families. We soon learned what poor confronters we were. For example, when a dog repeatedly turned over all our trash cans, we gossiped to each other about the problem instead of speaking with the dog's owner. And, yes, we threw rocks at the dog. The Holy Spirit convicted us of the sin of gossip, which we later defined as "giving one person a negative filter through which to view another."

Suppose I tell you that Mary Johnson was assigned to help me with cleanup after a large church social, but all she ever did was stand around and talk while I worked. If Mary Johnson is assigned to help you with cleanup next week, you will most likely see her through the negative filter I gave you. You would expect her to talk and not work. I don't know about you, but I have enough problems handling my own negative filters without handling yours as well.

Why then do we gossip?

- Gossip is less threatening than talking face to face with the problem person. We take what seems to be the easiest way out only to discover we've stepped into a hornet's nest of trouble.

- The story we retell is usually slanted to make us look good and the other person flawed. We fail to realize the damage we inflict on another's reputation.

- We try to manipulate people to join our side.

- We gain sympathy for ourselves by telling the dreadful way we have been treated.

- Gossip makes us feel powerful—we know something someone else does not know.

- We have poor communication skills and often don't know how to talk about a problem without making it worse.

What reasons are behind your own gossiping?

_____

_____

_____

_____

A Closer Look at God's Truth

WHAT SCRIPTURE SAYS ABOUT GOSSIP

Read Proverbs 16:28. What other problems are caused by gossip?

_____

_____

_____

_____

Read Proverbs 20:19. How are we to treat a gossip?

_____

_____

_____

_____

Read 2 Corinthians 12:20. What cluster of problems does Paul list along with gossip?

_____

_____

_____

Read 3 John 9-10. How did John handle gossip?

_____

_____

_____

_____

Scripture teaches us that gossip not only separates good friends but also brings anger, strife and quarreling. Gossip is the work of Satan and is a primary weapon he uses to destroy Christian fellowship.

Read Ephesians 4:15,25,29. If the people involved in the choir director's story had obeyed these verses, what hurts could have been avoided?

_____

_____

_____

_____

Give an example of when you have spoken in love, even when it may have hurt the listener. If you cannot think of an example of speaking in love, describe a time when you were afraid to confront someone. What were the results of not confronting that person?

_____

_____

_____

_____

Give an example of when you created a secondary problem by avoiding the first problem, as the pastor did. What happened as a result?

_____

_____

_____

_____

What do you think the pastor should have done when the first person complained to him about Miss Smith?

_____

_____

_____

_____

In one church, I've heard about how the staff members covenanted together to stop all gossip about church members and other staff members. Wow! That's a humbling yet powerful decision with the promise of the Holy Spirit revolutionizing and empowering the entire church. If you

sometimes or often speak to a third party about a problem person, instead
of to the person, pause now for a moment of prayer. Ask the Holy Spirit
to reveal the reasons behind your behavior.

WHAT SCRIPTURE SAYS ABOUT REBUKING
Read Psalms 39:11 and 50:16-21. When does God rebuke people?

_____
_____
_____
_____
_____

Read Proverbs 15:31-32. In what ways do these Scriptures encourage us to
rebuke when necessary?

_____
_____
_____
_____

According to Matthew 18:15-17, what is the godly way to rebuke a fellow
Christian?

_____
_____
_____
_____
_____

Read Matthew 23:23-36 and 1 Peter 2:21-23. What caused Jesus to give a
sharp rebuke in the first situation while in the second He remained silent?

_____
_____
_____
_____

Jesus sharply rebuked anyone who sinned against God or led others into
sin, but He never defended Himself against personal attack. This is a powerful position to take against others' rebukes of us. There are times to rebuke and times not to rebuke a fellow Christian.

Read Galatians 2:11-16; 1 Timothy 5:1,20; 2 Timothy 3:16; 4:2 and Titus 2:15. Invest time in reflecting on these Scriptures and summarize what you have learned about giving a rebuke.

_____

_____

_____

_____

_____

Before rebuking a sinner, we need to decide if his or her actions have drawn others into sin. Paul publicly rebuked Peter because others had followed his example of refusing to eat with Gentiles. This legalistic behavior could not be tolerated in the new church community.

Once we decide that a rebuke is in order, we then need to select the time, place and choice of words prayerfully. With non-inflammatory words, free of accusation and judgment, we must speak in a neutral tone of voice.

Poor: "You are a gossip and troublemaker. I am sick and tired of your causing dissension in the church."

Better: "Betty, I have some difficulty with what you just shared with me. I don't like to hear gossip. It gives me a negative view of my fellow Christians whom I'm supposed to love. Why don't you talk with this person and see if you can work things out between the two of you?"

If we compare the number of times in God's Word that we are told to love one another with the number of times that we are told to rebuke or admonish, we quickly see that Scripture emphasizes unconditional love. When we totally accept others in love and with prayers for the thorn in our side, the Holy Spirit is free to correct and convince the other person of thoughtless or sinful behavior. Our criticism usually changes no one.

We may challenge these instructions, pointing to the example of Jesus who rebuked sinners harshly. But He was God's Son—without sin! Let's rebuke in a way that gains an audience with the other person and makes it as easy as possible for him or her to repent.

What Scripture Says About Admonishing

How does an admonishment differ from a rebuke? The emphasis of a rebuke is for the listener to repent for an offense against God—"You have sinned." The emphasis of an admonishment is for the listener to heed a warning or earnest advice—"Let me tell you what the Bible says about this problem." The Greek word for "admonishment" means "a putting in mind." And with the help of the Holy Spirit, we are capable admonishers. Paul wrote:

> I myself am convinced, my brothers, that you yourselves are full of goodness, complete in knowledge and competent to instruct one another (Romans 15:14).

A Closer Look at My Own Heart

Think of a situation where you may need to admonish someone. Ask yourself each of the following questions about this situation. Decide what you should do about admonishing this person. What will you do about this situation this week?

- *Do I have the grace to overlook this behavior and not talk to anyone else about it?* If so, I will forgive and forget. Mary Johnson's unhelpful kitchen behavior could have been handled with a kind, upbeat admonishment, spoken directly to Mary: "Mary, I really need to finish with this cleanup and get home. Could you come and help?"

- *Will this person's behavior hurt only me?* If so, I will not admonish, remembering, "A man's wisdom gives him patience; it is to his glory to overlook an offense" (Proverbs 19:11).

- *What are my motives?* Do I have the other person's best interest at heart, or do I want to straighten out his or her behavior because I am irritated? If I cannot correct in love, I will not speak.

- *Is this an opportunity to forgive others as God forgives me?* Is my judging attitude the problem rather than the other person's behavior? If so, I will not speak.

Remember, gossip destroys fellowship; correction gains more favor than a flattering tongue. Let us speak the truth in love, knowing that we cannot protect people from pain. Pain is as much a part of relationships as laughter.

Action Steps I Can Take Today

Reread the reasons for gossip given in this chapter. Spend time in prayer, asking the Holy Spirit to bring to mind specific times when you have gossiped. As you reflect on these incidents, jot down possible motives.

If gossip is a sin in your life, you need to confess and repent. To repent does not mean to feel sorry for what you have done. (Of course, it's great if you do!) True repentance is a decision to stop, turn around and start walking in a new direction. It means that you realize the seriousness of your sin, and through God's empowerment you will turn your back on gossip and stop doing it.

If you have a repeated pattern of gossip, such as talking with your sister about your mother or talking with one coworker about another coworker, talk to the person with whom you most often share negatives. Tell him or her about your decision to stop gossiping, and ask this person to forgive you for involving him or her in gossip. Then ask the person to remind you of your decision if you slip up.

SIX

BEFRIENDING OUR EMOTIONS

As a Christian, have you ever condemned yourself for feeling angry at a friend, depressed about life, or indifferent toward reading the Bible or worshiping God? Many Christians are so uncomfortable with their emotions that they feel guilty when they feel anything but good. In this chapter, we'll learn the biblical way to handle our negative emotions by studying God's dealings with the emotions of Cain, David, Jonah and Job. We'll also learn to recognize that every person's emotional makeup is God's good gift; the "potting soil" in which relationships wither and die or take root and grow.

A Closer Look at the Problem

We can shut off our unwelcome thoughts by singing, praying, reading a good book or talking to a friend. We can decide to speak our thoughts or keep quiet. But try as we may, our feelings resist control. Joyous emotions escape like helium from a balloon, while our negative emotions burrow into the dark corners of our heart and resist all change. Life feels out of control when we can't control our (or others') emotions. Fear adds to our confusion.

We fear what others will think if our emotions are exposed. We don't want to look foolish or be judged childish. At the core of our fears are our basic misunderstandings about the role our emotions play in life. These are my three basic discoveries about emotions after decades of study:

1. *Emotions are our initial, involuntary response to a situation or person.*

2. *Emotions are neutral, neither good nor bad, right nor wrong, silly nor sensible.*

3. *Emotions resist change.* When we wish to feel happy, we may feel sad. When everyone wants to celebrate, we might feel like crying. Because we feel out of control when emotions won't obey our

commands, we sometimes build a thick inner wall of protection to keep us from feeling anything, or we bury unpleasant emotions deep in the pit of our stomachs—only to suffer from stomach acid. Either of these choices is dangerous because each has far-reaching future consequences:

- If we build up our wall to keep out certain emotions, we risk losing all emotions—pleasant or painful. We could shut down, unable to experience life to the fullest.

- Buried emotions refuse to stay buried. As author John Powell writes, "When I repress my emotions, my stomach keeps score."

Recall a time when someone else's emotions stimulated your anger or fear. How did you respond?

_____
_____
_____
_____

Recall a time when life felt out of control because you couldn't control your emotions. How did you respond?

_____
_____
_____
_____

A Closer Look at God's Truth

GOD'S ATTITUDE

If we take an overview of Scriptures dealing with emotions, we may be better able to accept our emotions as God's good gift to us. Read Genesis 4:2-8. Describe God's attitude toward Cain's emotions.

_____
_____
_____
_____

What warnings did God give Cain about his negative feelings?

_____

_____

_____

What does this passage teach us about how to handle emotions?

_____

_____

_____

_____

God did not condemn Cain for being angry and depressed. In fact, in questioning Cain about his emotions (see verse 6), God seemed to have wanted Cain to openly discuss his emotions. But Cain refused God's offer. Only after acknowledging Cain's emotions did God warn him that sin was knocking at his door.

Cain's emotions were not his sin, but how he chose to handle his emotions led him to sin. Instead of talking with God about his emotions, Cain chose to focus his anger on his brother (and probably accused Abel of causing his anger). When we refuse to own—take responsibility for—our emotions and blame another person, resentment intensifies, anger builds and we stop speaking to one another. In extreme cases we might verbally, or even physically, hurt the one we blame for making us feel so depressed and angry.

Ask God to search your heart and enable you to acknowledge anyone you resent at this time. What has happened as a result of your blaming this person for your emotions? (Has it led to separation, accusations, brooding, and so forth?)

_____

_____

_____

The healthiest way to handle emotions is to say "I am feeling angry" instead of "You make me angry." Which do you usually say?

_____

_____

_____

_____

Read Jonah 3:10–4:11. Did God condemn Jonah for being angry? What was God telling Jonah about his anger?

_____
_____
_____
_____

Do you think Jonah would have wanted to die if he had talked to God about his feelings? Explain your answer.

_____
_____
_____
_____

THE DEVIL'S FOOTHOLD

Read Ephesians 4:26-27. What does Paul tell us is the greatest danger we face when we have negative feelings toward another person?

_____
_____
_____
_____

Recall some times in your life when you held on to your anger and resentment and did not forgive the person who hurt you until days, weeks, months or years after the day of the emotional event. In what ways, if any, did the devil gain a foothold over your life during that time?

_____
_____
_____
_____

Read Mark 3:5; Luke 19:41 and John 13:21. List the emotions Jesus experienced in these passages.

_____
_____
_____
_____

Read Exodus 20:5 and Numbers 11:10. What are the two negative emotions God feels?

_____

_____

_____

_____

_____

What conclusions about emotions can you draw from reading these passages?

_____

_____

_____

_____

_____

BIBLICAL LESSONS

Here's my list of four biblical lessons about emotions.

1. *The fabric of life is woven with the warp and woof of positive and negative emotions.* We cannot expect to feel good all the time.

2. *The Bible does not condemn emotions.* The sin is not in the possession of emotions but in the expression and actions we take in response to our feelings.

3. *God encourages us to get our eyes off our problems and focus on Him who is the answer.* God wanted Cain and Jonah to talk with Him about their feelings, to express their emotions to the divine listener. If they had, they would most likely have been freed to live life above their anger and depression.

4. *We need negative emotions.* Fear keeps us from taking foolish risks. Depression may signal a need for withdrawal and rest. Anger is an indicator of possible problems. These emotions are signals, like red lights blinking on the dashboard of a car. They call us to stop and lift the "hoods" of our lives and let God examine us until we find out *why* we are experiencing

these emotions. We will then learn about our hidden problems of insecurity, rejection of self, resentment against God, bitterness, unforgiveness, lack of faith, and so forth.

Read Psalm 6. What emotions did David express to the Lord in this psalm?

_____

_____

_____

_____

When David expressed his emotions, what changes took place in his outlook?

_____

_____

_____

_____

Read Psalm 13. What emotions did David express in this psalm?

_____

_____

_____

_____

Both Psalm 6 and Psalm 13 begin with David feeling separated from God and end with his affirmation of knowing God had heard him. He moved from a man of sorrow, feeling forgotten by God, to become a man of celebration, singing to the Lord. Jot down any ideas that you learned from David that might help you handle your negative emotions easier.

_____

_____

_____

_____

When I'm angry, hurt, disappointed or sad about a relationship failure, I go to the Lord and pour out my negative emotions. Like David, I am blunt and colorful in describing in prayer to my heavenly Father exactly how I feel, I journal my feelings, and sometimes I write a psalm. Often my emotions dwindle in intensity. I take a deep breath of gratitude, rejoice and shout, "I'm free!" only to discover that the demon of resentment has returned, uninvited. I do not experience the same instantaneous change in my life as David did, but I believe the psalms condense days of anguish into a moment of expression. While on this earth, we'll never know for sure how many days of wrestling with God preceded the peace of God settling over David's heart.

Getting free of negative emotions is a process with me. Whenever old, negative emotions toward another person resurface, I use them to draw closer to God. Instead of condemning myself for this recurrence—which leads to separation from God—I repeatedly cry out to God, "Be my love for Susie. I'm bankrupt of warm feelings toward her. Please let Your love flow through me to her." I also may repeatedly pray the following simple prayer in the days, weeks and months that follow a negative encounter: "Lord, I choose not to become discouraged by the repetition of this prayer. Be my strength. I choose to rejoice that I'm using my negative emotions as a stepping stone to intimacy with and dependence upon my heavenly Father."

MINISTERING TO HURTING PEOPLE
Do you remember how Job, after losing all his flocks, his children, his money and his health, blurted out his overload of negative feelings to his three friends who had come to console him? He moaned:

> May the day of my birth perish! . . . May God above not care about it. Why did I not perish at birth, and die as I came from the womb? Why was I not hidden in the ground like a stillborn child? Why is light given to those in misery, and life to the bitter of soul? I have no peace, no quietness; I have no rest, but only turmoil (Job 3:3-4,11,16,20,26).

Then his three friends chided him. Eliphaz said:

> Your words have supported those who stumbled; you have strengthened faltering knees. But now trouble comes to you, and you are discouraged; it strikes you, and you are dismayed. Consider now: Who, being innocent, has ever perished? Where were the upright ever destroyed? As I have observed, those who plow evil and those who sow trouble reap it (Job 4:4-5,7-8).

Bildad remarked:

> How long will you say such things? Your words are a blustering wind. If you will look to God and plead with the Almighty, if you are pure and upright, even now he will rouse himself on your behalf and restore you to your rightful place (Job 8:2,5-6).

Zophar added:

> If you devote your heart to [God] and stretch out your hands to him, if you put away the sin that is in your hand and allow no evil to dwell in your tent, then you will lift up your face without shame; you will stand firm and without fear (Job 11:13-15).

Job blurted out to his friends, "You, however, smear me with lies; you are worthless physicians, all of you! If only you would be altogether silent! For you, that would be wisdom" (Job 13:4-5). In what ways did Job's friends compound his suffering?

_____

_____

_____

_____

_____

Have you ever been treated as Job was by his friends? Why do you think we fall into the trap of acting like Job's friends?

_____

_____

_____

_____

_____

How do you want to be treated when you're emotionally upset?

_____

_____

_____

God did not judge, criticize or correct Job's honest outpouring of every possible dark emotion a person could feel. However, God did chide Job's three friends for their judging words, saying, "I am angry with you, . . . because you have not spoken of me what is right, as my servant Job has. . . . Job will pray for you, and I will accept his prayer and not deal with you according to your folly" (Job 42:7-8).

God, the divine listener, is the model of how we are to respond to others' shared emotions. It is important that we allow people the full expression of their emotions without receiving judgmental or defensive replies from us.

A Closer Look at My Own Heart

Answer the following questions to yourself:

- *Do I tend to correct, criticize or sermonize others' emotions?*

- *Am I so uncomfortable in the face of honestly expressed emotions that I try to reason away the other person's emotions?*

- *Do I reveal my superior spirit when I sit in judgment of the person experiencing deep emotions?*

If you do any of the above, prayerfully read and reread the following summary about emotions:

Emotions that are fully expressed by a hurting person and understood by the listener lose their power over our lives. Emotions that are judged, criticized or corrected intensify and hang around, robbing us of peace and joy.

As we said in chapter 3, "listening for understanding requires death to self." Most of us listen to speak and to solve problems. The following illustration and exercise give you practice in listening for understanding.

If a child screams to her mother, "I hate my sister!" the child needs understanding, not sermonizing. If the mother says, "Nice girls don't hate their sisters," the child has learned that she is not nice. She has to handle guilt as well as anger. She may decide never again to tell her mother what she is feeling.

However, if the mother responds with sympathy, saying something like, "It must be hard to live with a sister you hate," the child may open up and share more information about her real problem. She might say, "I don't really hate Amy, but I'm so sick of her getting all the attention. I try and try and never get a part in the play or a solo at church." After the child has expressed her emotions and received a hug from her mother, she is once again ready to take on life with its emotional hurts. She may even want to pray with her mother and thank God for her sister.

Answer the remarks below without judging, criticizing or correcting.

Johnny [returning home from school]: "Everybody on the bus hates me!"

Your Accepting Response:

_____

_____

_____

_____

If you correct the child and say, "You know that's not true. Craig is your best buddy, and he rides home on the bus with you," Johnny might surprise you by throwing his books on the floor, rushing to his bedroom and slamming the door.

A depressed widow: "I want to die! Life is meaningless without Daniel."

Your Accepting Response:

_____

_____

_____

_____

If you say, "Now, Peggy, you know you have lots of important church work to give your life meaning," your friend may wish she had not shared her emotions with you. You are more sympathetic if you say, "I sense your terrible loneliness. After 20 years of marriage, it must be awful to come home to a dark, empty house each night."

Joe Bayly's poignant quote from his book *The Last Thing We Talk About* says it best:

> I was sitting, torn by grief. Someone came and talked to me of God's dealings, of why it happened, of hope beyond the grave. He talked constantly, he said things I knew were true. I was unmoved, except to wish he'd go away. He finally did. Another came and sat beside me for an hour or more, listened when I said something, answered briefly, prayed simply and left. I was moved. I was comforted. I hated to see him go.[1]

In summary, our emotions in themselves are neither right nor wrong, good nor bad. Sin lies in the way of expression, not in the possession, of emotions. When we are emotionally upset, we can avoid sinning by fully expressing our emotions to God in prayer or by writing psalms. We can also join God as one who listens to others' emotions without judging, correcting or criticizing. We can help our friends by accepting them with their negative emotions and empathize with them as Paul instructs us to do in Romans 12:15: "Rejoice with those who rejoice; mourn with those who mourn."

Action Steps I Can Take Today

In the light of this lesson, ask yourself the following questions:

- *Do I ever judge myself as less of a Christian because of what I feel?* If so, what has this lesson taught you that you need to apply today?

  _____

  _____

  _____

  _____

- *What difficulties do I have in accepting my emotional makeup as God's good gift to me?* Review God's attitude toward Cain, Jonah, David and Job, and then write down God's attitude toward emotions.

  _____

  _____

  _____

  _____

- *Which one of these reactions—criticism, correction or judgment—is my usual response to the emotions of others?* What can you do to improve in listening to others' emotions without criticism, correction or judgment?

  _____

  _____

  _____

  _____

- *What kind of listener do I want to be?* Write out a prayer to God to ask Him to work through you to make you a divine listener.

  _____

  _____

  _____

  _____

Note

1. Joseph Bayly, *The Last Thing We Talk About* (Elgin, IL: Chariot Family Publishing, 1992), p. 29.

LEARNING TO LISTEN

St. Francis of Assisi prayed, "Grant that I may not so much seek to be understood as to understand." Unfortunately we often seek the opposite. We prefer to speak, to tell our side of the story, to straighten out every detail of someone else's version of a story that differs ever so slightly from ours.

How do you receive criticism from your parents, your siblings, your spouse, your boss or your best friend? (Our defensiveness varies, depending on the person correcting or criticizing us and our relationship with that person.)

_____

_____

_____

_____

On a scale of 1 to 10 (with 10 being extremely self-defensive), how would you rate yourself as a non-defensive person? Why did you give yourself that rating?

_____

_____

_____

_____

I invite you to join me in praying the following:

Dear Lord Jesus,
I am often defensive when accused of wrongdoing. I know and use the weapons of denial and counterattack. I speak before listening fully to another's accusations. At times I let pride keep me separated from a friend. I delay humbling myself, admitting my wrong and asking to be forgiven. Lord Jesus, You humbled Yourself in leaving Your throne in heaven to become a man. Teach me humility, so I will freely acknowledge where I have been wrong and ask to be forgiven. Amen.

A Closer Look at the Problem

It doesn't matter if the "something" between two people is large or small, rational or irrational, important or unimportant. If a coolness exists between two members of the Body of Christ, their talking together is essential. And non-defensive listening is the skill most needed at a time like this.

I had to do this one night with a friend. We had both attended a neighborhood worship service held upstairs in our two-family home. When my neighbor's baby cried during those quiet moments of worship and reflection, I remembered that my 21-year-old son was downstairs watching television. I decided to take the baby to him. I walked across the room to where my neighbor stood worshiping, took the baby from her arms and whispered, "I'll take Katy to Craig." I didn't ask her permission and she said nothing. When I returned from delivering the baby to my son's care, I knew I was in trouble. My bubbly, joyful neighbor was scowling, inspecting the floor. I knew she had something against me. I rushed over to speak with her at the close of the meeting, but she rushed out the back door with Katy clutched in her arms.

I was tired and wanted to go to bed. But I knew the message of Matthew 5:23-24:

> Therefore, if you are offering your gift at the altar and there remember that your brother has something against you, leave your gift there in front of the altar. First go and be reconciled to your brother; then come and offer your gift.

My neighbor was one of those beautifully transparent people who shared her emotions openly. If I asked her to tell me how she was feeling, I knew she would. That's why I was going to help set her free of negative emotions by listening non-defensively. I had caused her pain and I was sorry. As I walked to her house, I rehearsed what I would say to her.

When we sat down to talk, a definite coolness filled the room. Nervously I opened the conversation by saying, "I know I have upset you. I've come to listen to you and try to understand how you felt when I snatched Katy from your arms." After my rehearsed introduction, my neighbor boiled over with her version of our encounter.

"You were thoughtless, Bobbie. You didn't stop to think about my feelings or ask me what I wanted done with my baby. You put me in an awkward position."

I felt a knot forming in my stomach, and I longed to shout, "That's not true! I was only trying to help." Instead, I managed to look calmly at my neighbor, swallow and say, "It must have been hard for you. I guess I did appear thoughtless." Notice that I agreed only with the part of my neighbor's speech that was true for me, instead of trying to correct her or defend myself.

"I was ready to take Katy home tonight when you snatched her from my arms. She was tired and needed to go to bed. She didn't need to be taken downstairs to Craig. You know she's afraid of men with beards."

I didn't know that men's beards frightened her baby. Again I wanted to defend myself, explain my innocence. I resisted with increased determination.

"I feel you were punishing your son, not helping me," my neighbor accused.

I thought, *My friend, that's enough. You've gone too far.* Instead I miraculously managed to respond to my neighbor's accusation, again accepting the part that was true for me. "I never thought of it that way. You may be right. I was mad at my son," I agreed. "Will you forgive me for my insensitivity and thoughtlessness?" I asked.

With a twinkle in her eyes, my neighbor reached out, hugged me and offered me a cup of coffee. I stayed and talked and went home delightfully free, knowing that for once in my life I had obeyed Jesus' command in Luke 9:23-24: "If anyone would come after me, he must deny himself and take up his cross daily and follow me. For whoever wants to save his life will lose it, but whoever loses his life for me will save it."

If you had kept a tally of points scored, I would have lost. But in losing I won back a friend, practiced humility, learned to listen non-defensively and felt so happy that I skipped home. The art of such non-defensive listening has three requirements, each of which is difficult to master but certainly worth the investment of time and discipline:

1. *Put down pride.* We humble ourselves, admit our wrongs without excusing them and ask to be forgiven. The Bible commands us to "be completely humble and gentle; be patient, bearing with one another in love" (Ephesians 4:2). Someone has said, "To be right satisfies my ego; to be humble satisfies God." In giving my friend the gift of non-defensive listening, I felt as if I had satisfied God.

2. *Refuse to correct.* The object of non-defensive listening is to be able to say, "I understand why you feel that way," not "You're wrong. It never happened that way." We are able to receive the other person's version of what happened when we realize that feelings are neither right nor wrong. The shared feelings are true only to the sharer. My neighbor later confided to me that our conversation was the first time in her life that anyone had fully listened to her outpouring of negative emotions. She said that she was uptight and angry when I walked in but totally free of all negative emotions when I walked out. Think of the lovely gift we can give to someone when we practice non-defensive listening—when we release self-defense and embrace humility.

3. *Cancel all counterattacks.* When we are criticized or corrected, our natural response is to counterattack: "Who do you think you are criticizing my tone of voice when you sound like an angry bulldog most of the time." This does not conform to the Bible's teachings:

> But love your enemies, do good to them, and lend to them without expecting to get anything back. Then your reward will be great, and you will be sons of the Most High, because he is kind to the ungrateful and wicked. Be merciful, just as your Father is merciful (Luke 6:35-36).

A Closer Look at God's Truth

Read Luke 15:18-20. The parable of the prodigal son recounts how a young man returned home to be forgiven after squandering all his inheritance. Before reaching his father's home, he had carefully planned and practiced what he would say to his father. What approach was he going to take?

_____

_____

_____

_____

_____

Contemplate how this young man approached his need for forgiveness. How does he inspire you to make changes in how you handle forgiveness?

_____

_____

_____

_____

The prodigal son's concern centered not on himself but on his father and the pain he had caused him. When we have wronged others, we need to go quickly to them to seek restoration, not exoneration. If we want them to tell us we are still okay, we are excused. But if we want them to tell us that it wasn't that important, then we are seeking exoneration. In such cases, we want to make up, bypass the problem and skip talking about it.

Exoneration, like making up, is external. Restoration, on the other hand, is internal and brings healing. It centers on the relationship between two people and the harm done to that relationship by one's thoughtlessness or sin. The offender comes in humility to say, "I was wrong. I've hurt you and our relationship, and I need you to forgive me." When forgiven by the one offended, the offender knows he or she is accepted in his or her sin, and restoration happens.

Read Matthew 5:23-24. What premium does God place on reconciliation?

_____

_____

_____

If you procrastinate in asking for forgiveness, what additional problems might you create for yourself?

_____

_____

_____

_____

What do Proverbs 18:13 and James 1:19 have to say about listening?

_____

_____

_____

_____

What character weaknesses might our tongue reveal about ourselves?

_____

_____

_____

_____

A Closer Look at My Own Heart

Describe a time when you put self-protection above the pain you caused another person.

_____

_____

_____

_____

When was the last time you said to someone, "I was wrong. I need you to forgive me"? How difficult was it to say? What was the outcome?

_____

_____

_____

_____

What prevents you from saying "Forgive me" more often?

_____

_____

_____

_____

Action Steps I Can Take Today

Write a defensive and then a non-defensive reply to each of the following accusations. Remember to respond to the part of the accusation that is true for you.

A Coworker: "You were thoughtless yesterday. You embarrassed me when you corrected my spelling in front of the boss."

Defensive Response:

_____

_____

_____

_____

_____

Non-defensive Response:

_____

_____

_____

_____

_____

A Daughter: "You don't care about me. I don't matter. Tommy gets to do anything he wants, and I never get to do anything!"

Defensive Response:

_____

_____

_____

_____

Non-defensive Response:

_____

_____

_____

_____

A Friend: "I guess I don't matter to you anymore. You haven't asked me to be your golf partner for months, yet you've played with Jeff several times in the last few months."

Defensive Response:

_____

_____

_____

_____

Non-defensive Response:

_____

_____

_____

_____

Become aware this week of the way you reply to criticism or correction. Examine yourself daily. If you have given a defensive reply, reflect on the encounter and write a non-defensive reply. Include the prayer of St. Francis of Assisi on the first page of this lesson in your daily prayers as you ask God to make you one who listens without counterattacking.

EIGHT

GROWING IN GRACE

If we want to be persons of grace, we must follow the instructions Jesus gave in the Sermon on the Mount:

> You have heard that it was said, "Eye for eye, and tooth for tooth." But I tell you, Do not resist an evil person. If someone strikes you on the right cheek, turn to him the other also. And if someone wants to sue you and take your tunic, let him have your cloak as well. If someone forces you to go one mile, go with him two miles. Give to the one who asks you, and do not turn away from the one who wants to borrow from you. You have heard that it was said, "Love your neighbor and hate your enemy." But I tell you: Love your enemies and pray for those who persecute you (Matthew 5:38-44).

We cannot begin to obey these commandments without a big attitude adjustment, which is called "renewing of the mind" in the Bible: "Do not conform any longer to the pattern of this world, but be transformed by the renewing of your mind. Then you will be able to test and approve what God's will is—his good, pleasing and perfect will" (Romans 12:2).

In the lesson on emotions in chapter 6, we stated that the way we deal with our emotions is a frequent source of people problems. This is true. However, it is not the place to begin when we want to grow in grace and in our ability to respond lovingly to unlovely people. The place to begin is with our thought life. Today, most psychologists agree that emotions flow from our cognitions (our thoughts). We do not feel first and then think; we think first and then feel.

If you saw a snake in the road in front of you, coiled and ready to strike, what would you feel? Why would you feel that way?

_____

_____

_____

Your response to the snake would be determined by your self-talk, the things you say to yourself, and based on the things you have learned over the years. If you thought, *Snakes are dangerous; this snake might kill me,* you would experience the emotion of fear and run for your life. If you were a scientist, however, and thought, *I want to check this snake out—I must get closer and examine its markings and head shape,* you would experience the emotions of excitement and anticipation of learning more about snakes.

This final chapter will stress scriptural thinking as a necessity for right relationships. If we have problem people in our lives, the good news is that we can change the way we *feel* about them by changing the way we *think* about them. In changing the way we think, we adjust our attitude, words and actions and grow as people of grace, capable of returning good for evil.

If we believe that we feel first and then think, we are helpless to change our resentments toward our parents, our anger toward our employers, our disapproval of our pastor, our fear of heights, our jealousy of others' successes, or our depression because we haven't fulfilled our dreams. But since life is determined by what we think, we can always change our emotions. We have ready access to our thought life.

A Closer Look at the Problem

How would you define the New Testament word "grace"?

_____
_____
_____
_____
_____

There is a richness and depth in this word that we may never fully comprehend. *Vine's Expository Dictionary of New Testament Words* says:

> Grace . . . [is] the friendly disposition from which the kindly act proceeds, graciousness, loving-kindness, goodwill generally . . . especially with reference to the Divine favor of "grace." . . . There is stress on its freeness and universality, its spontaneous character, as in the case of God's redemptive mercy, and the pleasure of joy He designs for the recipient.[1]

To me, grace is giving love to the unlovely, forgiveness to the unforgivable, mercy to the unmerciful. In other words, grace is giving a person what he or she does not deserve, which, of course, is how God treats us. God's treatment of Manasseh, king of Judah, is a prime example of divine mercy.

Read 2 Chronicles 33:1-6,10-13. What did Manasseh do to deserve God's judgment?

_____

_____

_____

_____

_____

In spite of Manasseh's rejection of God, what did God do for him?

_____

_____

_____

_____

_____

Describe how you treat people who have ignored, hurt or misused you.

_____

_____

_____

_____

When it comes to people problems, the Bible shows us that we usually respond in one of three ways:

1. Like Paul, we ask God to remove the problem (see 2 Corinthians 12:7-10).

2. Like Adam and Eve, we blame others for our troubles (see Genesis 3:11-13).

3. Like Jonah, we try to run away from God (see Jonah 1:1-3). We may also try to escape from the people and from the problems created by their presence.

A fourth common way we respond to relationship rifts is to avoid the person giving us trouble. If people have mistreated us, we want to hurt them back and often do so by avoiding them. Ever so subtly (we think), we sit on the opposite side of the church, walk down another aisle in the supermarket or turn our back and talk to others at a gathering.

How quickly we want to escape our people problems. We want the people removed from our lives or to blame them for our discomfort. All four of these behaviors, however, help us grow in *disgrace*. (Remember, grace is giving others the kindness they do not deserve.) What God wants is for us to look to Him and ask, "Father, what am I to learn from this situation? How can I grow in grace toward those who have hurt me?"

Peter wrote about the total destruction of the earth and the believer's anticipation of a new heaven and a new earth. Since this is our hope, Peter challenges us to "grow in the grace and knowledge of our Lord and Savior Jesus Christ" (2 Peter 3:18).

A Closer Look at God's Truth

We have said in previous lessons that God's main concern is that we learn to react to our emotions in a godly way. That's why the first step toward becoming a person of grace is taking charge of our thought life, which leads to a change in our attitude.

Read Philippians 4:8. List the things Christians are called to think about.

_____

_____

_____

When we place our thoughts through the grid of this verse, most of us will agree that we need a mental overhaul. The Bible uses strong action words to let us know how much hard work and discipline are involved in changing our thought patterns. List some of the biblical commandments about our minds found in the following passages:

Romans 12:2

_____

_____

_____

Ephesians 4:23

_____
_____
_____
_____

Colossians 3:2

_____
_____
_____
_____

1 Peter 1:13

_____
_____
_____
_____

After reading these commands, we see that the Bible insists we can change our thinking by hard work and discipline.

THE LIES
A large percentage of what we think flies in the face of biblical truth, is sinful and is unacceptable to God. Too often we let Satan's lies replace God's truths.

The Lie: When people act unfairly, unkindly, thoughtlessly or obnoxiously, I should blame them and dwell on the wrong done to me or to others.

The Truth: (Use Romans 12:14,17-18 and Ephesians 4:31-32 to rewrite Satan's lie into scriptural truth.)

_____
_____
_____
_____
_____

The Lie: When I am rejected, hurt or unfairly treated, I have a right to be in a bad mood and harbor negative thoughts.

The Truth: (Use Matthew 5:11-12 to rewrite this lie into scriptural truth.)

_____

_____

_____

_____

The Lie: I have a right to criticize and judge other Christians when they fail to obey God's laws. When they don't, I should be depressed.

The Truth: (Use Matthew 7:1-5 and Galatians 6:1-2 to rewrite this lie into scriptural truth.)

_____

_____

_____

_____

The Lie: I have a right to expect people to remember me, give me gifts and do special things for me. When they don't, I should be depressed.

The Truth: (Use Philippians 2:3 to rewrite this lie into scriptural truth.)

_____

_____

_____

_____

The Lie: I expect people to listen to what's on my mind.

The Truth: (Use James 1:19,26 to rewrite this lie into scriptural truth.)

_____

_____

_____

_____

MENTAL REVENGE MOVIES

If we want healthy relationships, we must discipline our thoughts according to scriptural truth. But all too often when we have been hurt, snubbed, criticized or overlooked, our old natures scream for revenge. In our mind we create dramas based on past painful events. We are the stars of our dramas and have the best lines. We *mentally* "tell off" people who have hurt us and punish those who have caused us pain. The problem intensifies when our mental movies become reruns and then our favorite late-night shows. Consequently, our emotions match our thoughts, and we become plagued with negative, hostile feelings.

If you produce emotional home movies in your mind or lose sleep over your late-night shows, what can you do to stop the negative, get-even thinking?

_____
_____
_____
_____
_____
_____

When we find ourselves constantly rehashing the same painful memories, it is not helpful to tell ourselves, *I won't think that again.* In fact, when we tell ourselves we won't think certain things, we have just thought them a second time. Since our emotions and actions flow from our thoughts, we must be "made new in the attitude of [our] minds" (Ephesians 4:23).

A HEALTHY THOUGHT LIFE

The life of King David illustrates important principles for a healthy thought life with positive emotions and good relationships.

Read Psalm 42:1-3 and list the emotions that David was feeling.

_____
_____
_____
_____
_____
_____

Read Psalm 42:9-10 and describe David's attitude toward God.

_____

_____

_____

_____

Read Psalm 42:4-6 and list what David chose to think about, even in his depressed emotional state.

_____

_____

_____

_____

Notice three things about David's thoughts and words:

1. He unabashedly poured out his emotions to God. In telling God exactly how he felt, he seemed to know God as the divine listener of the universe who accepted him with his raw emotions without judging him as flawed.

2. He carefully edited his thought life, choosing to use *replacement thinking*. When he wanted to dwell on his plight in life at the hands of his enemies, he chose instead to remember happy, joyful times of celebrating God.

3. While David seemed to talk freely with God and say exactly how he felt, his self-talk was disciplined and carefully worded. He spoke sharply to his soul, demanding a walk of faith.

We see that when David chose to think of pure, good and true things, his emotions changed. He became a man of hope, knowing he would praise God again as he did in leading the festive procession.

REPLACEMENT THINKING

We cannot think about two things simultaneously. This is why replacement thinking proves effective. Instead of saying, "I won't think that again," we need to lift our negative thoughts to God and pray something like the following:

Father, I am thinking fearful, negative thoughts again. I give these thoughts to You and ask Your forgiveness for my lack of faith. I repent and choose to think on _____.

It is helpful to decide in advance what you will do when negative thoughts become repetitive. You might choose to pray about your church, about every member of your family, about your office staff, or whatever subject is important to you at the time. You might decide to praise God for all His spiritual and temporal blessings. You might quote Psalm 23 or some other memorized verses. Notice that I am not saying that you will never again have negative thoughts, but when negative thoughts come, you can replace them with positive, scriptural truth. You can use replacement thinking.

Another way to destroy our mental revenge movies is to challenge each thought according to Philippians 4:8. One way to do this is by asking ourselves the following:

Is this thought noble, right, pure or lovely? Is this thought admirable, excellent or praiseworthy? If not, I will choose to think on _____.

The Upward and Downward Spirals of Life

Study the following upward and downward spirals. What are their similarities? What are their differences?

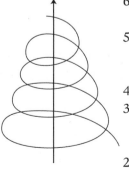

6   RELATIONSHIP IS RESTORED, becoming healthy again.

5   MOVEMENT IS TOWARD the person; we exhibit kindness, conversation, love and a request to be forgiven.

4   FORGIVENESS FLOWS and healing occurs.

3   POSITIVE MINDSET develops with a rehearsal of Scripture, prayer and praise. The results are the positive emotions of peace, faith and joy.

2   TRUST GOD to be at work in the situation.

1   CHOOSE to see the person and/or problem as God-sent.

PROBLEM

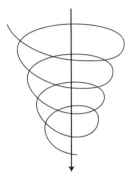

1. CHOOSE to see and/or think of a person or problem as an unfair, unwelcome intrusion.
2. MISTRUST GOD and His love and care.
3. NEGATIVE MINDSET develops with a rehearsal of details, role-plays and revenge movie scripts. The results are the negative emotions of bitterness, anger, depression, resentment and self-pity.
4. FORGIVENESS IS WITHHELD and wounds fester.
5. MOVEMENT IS AWAY from person; we indulge in gossip, waiting for person to ask forgiveness, and blindness to our own wrongs.
6. RELATIONSHIP BREAKS, causing emotional and mental pain, sometimes accompanied by physical sickness.

If we do not use replacement thinking and challenge our thoughts when we've been hurt or mistreated, we can get into a downward spiral. If we choose to see the person or problem as God-sent and we reaffirm our faith in God, we will experience an upward spiral.

These upward and downward spirals remind us that no matter what happens to us, we can choose how we will respond and think. Time is involved in both spirals; attitudes develop, feelings are affected, and relationships are decided.

A Closer Look at My Own Heart

Study the upward and downward spirals. Where do you see victory in your life?

_____

_____

_____

_____

_____

_____

Where do you see defeat?

_____
_____
_____
_____
_____

Pinpoint the step that causes you to stumble into a downward spiral.

_____
_____
_____
_____
_____

To be people of grace, we must reach out to others even as they reject us; do deeds of kindness to the ones who hurt us; and refuse to be separated from the rest of the Body.

Separation of friends is the work of Satan. He knows that if he can keep friends apart long enough, healing will not happen. The longer the separation, the more emotional home movies we produce. Distorted thinking develops. The problem people become monsters in our minds. We come to believe that these people not only hurt us once but also that they are out to destroy us.

Replacement thinking is one solution to distorted thinking. Another solution is to reach out to the ones we most want to avoid. We can call them on the phone, stop by to talk, share a meal or take them a small memento of one of the good times we've spent together. It's vital that we do whatever it takes to bring us face to face with the one against whom we hold a grudge. Amazingly, the longer we spend time together the quicker negative feelings dissolve.

Have you let a relationship grow cool because you were hurt? Based on this lesson, what steps will you take to try to restore the relationship with the one who hurt you?

_____
_____
_____
_____

List any problem people that you need to accept as God's good gift to you.

_____

_____

_____

_____

Action Steps I Can Take Today

Use the worksheet on the following page to determine what actions you need to take to restore a broken relationship.

Note

1. W. E. Vine, *Vine's Expository Dictionary of New Testament Words* (Uhrichsville, OH: Barbour & Company, Inc., 1985).

ℛELATIONSHIP WORKSHEET

1. Stop and pray, "Lord, show me anyone in my family, my church, my neighborhood, my office or factory who I am avoiding. Am I cool toward anyone in my life?" Wait upon the Holy Spirit and listen expectantly. Write down the name of the person who comes to mind.

   _____

2. Stop and check yourself: *Have I forgiven this person for his or her thoughtlessness or insensitivity to me? Have I prayed a specific prayer of forgiveness, naming the person by name and specifying the hurt to be forgiven?*

   ❑ Yes   ❑ No

   Note: Do not move on until you can answer yes to question 2.

3. Ask the Lord to show you one act of kindness you can do for this person you feel like avoiding. (It may be anything from baking a cake to sitting by the person at the next choir rehearsal.) Pray this prayer:

   Lord Jesus, I ask that You show me one loving act that I can do for
   _____ (name of person).

   Wait upon the Lord until you decide on one definite act of kindness to help you actively express your new feelings.

4. Make a decision to do this action as soon as possible, trusting in the power of the Holy Spirit to show love through you.

   I will _____
   (name of action) for _____
   (name of person) on _____ (date).

5. Decide today to ask forgiveness for allowing a rift to develop between you and the person who you feel wronged you. Go as a humbled person to be forgiven, not as a wronged person to be heard. Think about what you are going to say. Write out your request below.

   _____
   _____
   _____

Practice saying your request, so you can go in humility.

BUILDING BETTER RELATIONSHIPS LEADER'S GUIDE

The purpose of this leader's guide is to provide those willing to lead a group Bible study with additional material to make the study more effective. Each lesson has one or two exercises designed to increase participation and lead the group members into a more conscious awareness of the effects of worry on their lives.

Each of the exercises are designed to introduce the study and emphasize the theme of the chapter. When two exercises are suggested, it is up to your discretion whether to use them both. Time will probably be the deciding factor.

If the group is larger than six members, you may want to break into smaller groups for the discussion time so that all will have an adequate opportunity to share. As the lessons proceed, the exercises will invite more personal sharing. Keep these two important points in mind:

1. Involve each member of the group in the discussion when at all possible. Some may be too shy or new to the Bible study experience. Be sensitive to their needs and encourage them to answer simple questions that do not require personal information or biblical knowledge. As they get more comfortable in the group, they will probably share more often.

2. Make a commitment with the group members that what is shared in the discussion times and prayer requests must be kept in strictest confidence.

After each lesson, be prepared to pray with those who have special needs or concerns. Emphasize the truth of God's Word as you minister to the group members. Expect Him to begin to heal the broken relationships in their lives and empower them to reach out and build right relationships.

$\mathscr{B}$UILDING RIGHT RELATIONSHIPS

Objective

To help group members understand *agapao* love and how to apply it in their relationships.

Preparation

EXERCISE

Obtain several sheets of 9" x 12" red construction paper or poster board, enough for at least one piece for each group member. Cut out several large hearts from the paper or poster board (or you might be able to purchase a package of large hearts from a party supply or craft store). Gather several black ink felt-tip pens.

DISCUSSION

Familiarize yourself with the questions in the "A Closer Look at God's Truth" section and the participant self-test in the "A Closer Look at My Own Heart" section. Note that there might not be time to discuss every question, so modify or adapt this discussion guide as it fits the needs of your group.

Group Participation

EXERCISE

Give each group member a large paper heart and a felt-tip pen. Discuss the differences between God's view of love and the world's view of love. Ask the group members to write a brief completion to the statement, "Human love is . . ." on one side of the heart. Invite the group members to share the different aspects of human love that they have written down. Ask them what kinds of things can make those kinds of love go sour (for example, a romance breaks up, the spouse has an affair, a family member hurts you, a friend betrays you, the charity is bogus, and so forth). Instruct group members to turn their hearts over and then write their brief responses to the statement, "God's love is . . ." Discuss the differences between God's love and human expressions of love.

DISCUSSION
1. Begin the discussion by inviting group members to share their definitions of right relationships.

2. Invite group members to share the key action words they listed for each of the verses on page 20. After each shared answer, ask the group to suggest practical actions that can be taken to demonstrate the action. For example, one answer to the first statement for Romans 12:10, might be "be devoted" to one another. An action that might be suggested is "spend time in fellowship with fellow believers." (Note that this question has two possible answers: "be devoted to one another" and "show honor to one another." Accept both answers.) Continue down the list as time allows.

3. Discuss the groups' answers to the question "What are some of the reasons you find it difficult to maintain right relationships?" Don't ask group members to share specific people, but just have them share in general those things that make it difficult or easy to maintain right relationships.

4. Ask the members what they discovered about themselves when they rated themselves in the area of their relationships. In what areas did they find they needed to grow in obedience to God's relationship commandments?

ADDITIONAL DISCUSSION/ACTION STEPS
Invite volunteers to share any action steps they have taken as a result of this week's lesson.

TWO

*L*OVING OUR NEIGHBORS

Objective

To guide group members to understand what it means to love their neighbors.

Preparation

EXERCISE 1
Obtain lined paper and pens or pencils.

DISCUSSION
Familiarize yourself with the discussion questions included in the following "Group Participation" section, or choose which questions in this week's study you want to discuss with the group.

Group Participation

EXERCISE 1
Read the story of The Good Samaritan from Luke 10:30-36. Divide the group into smaller groups of three to four and give them lined paper and pens or pencils. Instruct the small groups to develop their own parable of a present-day Good Samaritan. After about 15 minutes, invite the groups to share their parables. Discuss the following questions related to the Good Samaritan parable:

1. Who might each of the characters relate to in modern-day life? (*Priest: religious people; Levites: professionals who are supposed to help others, such as lawyers, doctors, police; the Samaritan: the outcasts of our culture, such as the homeless, the poor, or others who don't "fit in"; the victim: anyone in need.*)

2. In what ways do we as Christians respond as the Good Samaritan did?

3. In what ways don't we respond as Jesus would want us?

4. Invite group members to share a time they: (a) were aided by a Good Samaritan; (b) acted as a Good Samaritan; or (c) should have been a Good Samaritan and did not help someone.

DISCUSSION

1. Discuss the following questions (or the ones you chose) from the "A Closer Look at God's Truth" section:

    • What does 1 John 3:14-15 say about the seriousness of our relationships with one another? How do you feel as you read this Scripture?

    • Read 1 John 3:16-18. What is the one sure way we know that God loves us?

    • Write a definition of love that includes biblical truth on this subject.

2. Discuss the following questions (or the ones you chose) from the "A Closer Look at My Own Heart" section:

    • Read Luke 9:23-24. What does it mean to you to take up your cross daily?

    • Write a definition of self-denial.

    • Read John 13:34-35 and Romans 13:8-10. List the reasons for loving your neighbors as you love yourself.

ADDITIONAL DISCUSSION/ACTION STEPS

Invite volunteers to share any action steps they have taken as a result of this week's lesson.

*H*ONORING ONE ANOTHER

Objective

To help group members understand what God means when He commands us to honor others.

Preparation

EXERCISE 1

Compile lists of the latest winners of Hollywood awards shows, Nobel prizes, sports awards, and so forth. If possible, cut out pictures of celebrities, sports figures, politicians or others who have won some of these awards or who have been honored for their achievements. Prepare to display them at your meeting place by taping or gluing the photos to poster board, or tack them on a bulletin board.

EXERCISE 2

Develop four or five comments similar to those on pages 39-40 for group members to use in practicing the Three Q Test and respectful responses. Write each comment on an index card. Also bring blank index cards and pens or pencils.

DISCUSSION

Familiarize yourself with the discussion questions included in the following "Group Participation" section, or choose which questions in this week's study you want to discuss with the group.

Group Participation

EXERCISE 1

Display the photos of the celebrities, sports figures, politicians and others that you have gathered. Read the lists you have compiled of this year's winners for various awards. Ask group members if they can remember who won these honors in previous years. There might be a few people in the group who can remember some of the names, but by and large most cannot. Discuss the following:

1. In what ways are the people in these photos honored? Why do we know who they are? In what ways are they worthy of the honor and attention they receive?

2. Who are some people who should be honored but whose existence or importance is usually not typically acknowledged in our culture? (*Stay-at-home mothers, parents who work hard to take care of their families, single parents, caretakers of the elderly or disabled, and so forth.* You could also encourage them to list people who have jobs who are not often honored, such as *custodians, sales clerks, farm workers, truckers, and the like.*)

3. How does the church fall into the honoring-celebrities trap? What can happen to celebrity Christians?

4. What are some practical ways according to the Bible that we as believers can show honor to those who truly deserve it?

EXERCISE 2

Divide the group into smaller groups of two to four. (Note: If your entire group has fewer than six members, have them work on this project together.) Hand each group one or two of the index cards that you have prepared ahead of time, and also give each group one or two blank index cards. Instruct the groups to develop three questions they could ask in response to the comments listed on their index cards. Ask them to give an example of a disrespectful answer and then a respectful answer.

Instruct them to be prepared to role-play their responses (they can prepare by writing their responses on the blank index cards). Give them about 8 to 10 minutes to complete this assignment, and then call the whole group back together to share their responses. To role-play their responses, have one member make the initial comment, and then have the other small-group members take turns asking the three Qs, giving a disrespectful answer and then the respectful answer.

DISCUSSION

1. Read this quote from chapter 3: "When we honor others, we are honoring their Creator. When we dishonor others, we dishonor God." Ask the members if they agree or disagree. Have them explain their answers.

2. As time allows, discuss the following questions (or the ones you chose) from the "A Closer Look at God's Truth" section:

    *   Read John 14:13; 15:26 and 17:24 and record how the members of the Godhead glorify each other.

    *   What are some specific things you might do to call attention to others, as the members of the Godhead do for one another?

    *   Read Romans 12:10. Whom should you honor?

    *   In the world's view, what things make a person worthy of honor?

    *   Read Genesis 1:26-27 and Psalm 8:3-9 and compare the world's reasons for honoring others with God's reasons for honoring all people.

3. Ask the members to list some of the ways they would welcome Jesus if He dropped by during this Bible study.

ADDITIONAL DISCUSSION/ACTION STEPS

Invite volunteers to share any action steps they have taken as a result of this week's lesson.

ℰNCOURAGING ONE ANOTHER

Objective

To guide group members to understand the value of others and the command from God to encourage one another.

Preparation

EXERCISE 1

Obtain as many different Bible translations as possible. Write the following Scripture references on a whiteboard, chalkboard or flipchart: John 11:19; 1 Thessalonians 5:11; Hebrews 3:13; John 14:16; Acts 4:36; 2 Corinthians 1:3.

EXERCISE 2

Gather note cards with envelopes and pens.

DISCUSSION

Familiarize yourself with the discussion questions included in the following "Group Participation" section, or choose which questions in this week's study you want to discuss with the group.

Group Participation

EXERCISE 1

(Note: This is a good exercise to do if you believe many of your group members might not possess several different Bible translations.) Hand out each Bible translation to a group member. Invite those who have the Bibles to look up the verse and then read it aloud. Invite the group members to call out the different words that are used to translate *parakaleo/paraklesis*. Record the words next to the appropriate Scripture verse on the whiteboard, chalkboard or flipchart. Ask the members how these different words help them understand how to encourage others. Based on these Scriptures, what do they think the Bible means when it tells us to "encourage" one another daily?

DISCUSSION

1. Discuss the following questions from the "A Closer Look at God's Truth" section:

   - Read Genesis 3:14-15,21 and Revelation 21:1-4. In what ways do these Scriptures comfort you?

   - Read Hebrews 3:12-13. Why is it crucial to encourage others daily?

2. Discuss the following questions from the "A Closer Look at My Own Heart" section:

   - Read Ephesians 4:29. Place the stethoscope of this verse to your heart and ask God to reveal any negative patterns of unwholesome speech that you might have, such as gossip, anger, put-downs or joking at the expense of others. Write down those times.

   - Ask God to also reveal times when you have failed to encourage others. Write down those times.

ADDITIONAL DISCUSSION/ACTION STEPS

1. How has someone encouraged you this week?

2. How have you encouraged another person this week? What was that person's reaction?

3. What action step(s) did you take this past week? What were the results?

4. What action step(s) are you resolved to take in encouraging others during this coming week?

EXERCISE 2

At the close of this session, give each group member a note card with an envelope and a pen. Invite them to write a note of encouragement to someone. It could be a fellow group member, a friend, family member, a church member—anyone whom they know could use encouragement. Give them a few moments to write the note, and then instruct them to take it home and mail it or personally deliver it to the person. Ask them to be prepared to share about the experience next week.

FIVE

HANDLING CONFRONTATION

Objective

To identify the sin of gossip and its effects on communication with others, and also to help group members recognize the value, the proper time and the attitude for healthy confrontation.

Preparation

EXERCISE 2

Collect a few popular gossip magazines. Try to have one for every three to four members in the group.

DISCUSSION

Familiarize yourself with the discussion questions included in the following "Group Participation" section, or choose which questions in this week's study you want to discuss with the group.

Group Participation

EXERCISE 1

Invite group members to share about the responses they received from those to whom they had sent the notes of encouragement.

EXERCISE 2

Begin by discussing why we love to gossip. Divide the group into smaller groups of three to four people each. Give each group a gossip magazine. Instruct the groups to find one story in the magazine to discuss. Instruct them to read the story and to imagine that they are the person the article is written about. Have the small groups discuss the ramifications that this story would have on the people involved, on their families and friends, and on those who idolize these people. Bring the group together and have them summarize their discoveries about the damage that gossip can cause.

Discussion

1. Discuss the following questions (or the ones you chose) from the "A Closer Look at God's Truth" section:

    - Read Proverbs 16:28. What other problems are caused by gossip?

    - Read Proverbs 20:19. How are we to treat a gossip?

    - Read 2 Corinthians 12:20. What cluster of problems does Paul list along with gossip?

    - Read 3 John 9-10. How did John handle gossip?

    - Give an example of when you have spoken in love, even when it may have hurt the listener. If you cannot think of an example of speaking in love, describe a time when you were afraid to confront someone. What were the results of not confronting that person?

    - Give an example of when you created a secondary problem by avoiding the first problem, as the pastor did. What happened as a result?

    - According to Matthew 18:15-17, what is the godly way to rebuke a fellow Christian?

    - Read Galatians 2:11-16; 1 Timothy 5:1,20; 2 Timothy 3:16; 4:2 and Titus 2:15. Invest time in reflecting on these Scriptures and summarize what you have learned about giving a rebuke.

Additional Discussion/Action Steps

1. Ask if there is anyone who has ever had to confront someone about a problem lately. What was the result? (Note: Caution those who share to be careful not to include any information that would identify the person. Ask them to speak in general terms about the incident.)

2. Ask the group the biblical principles there are for confronting another person about his or her behavior (see Matthew 18:15-17). Remind group members that confrontation should only be done after much prayer.

3. Ask members what they can do when the person they confront is not very receptive and becomes angry.

4. Close the meeting by inviting anyone who has a need to confront someone to be prayed for by the group members. Once again, remind the group members to not refer to the person to be confronted by name or relationship, but in general terms. Pray that the confronter would have the wisdom and discernment to know the right time and place, and that the Lord would guide his or her words. Pray for a receptive heart on the part of the one being confronted.

SIX

$\mathscr{B}$EFRIENDING OUR EMOTIONS

Objective

To help group members understand that emotions need to be expressed and that there are biblically acceptable ways to express those emotions. Also, to guide them in appropriate, healthy responses to the emotions expressed by others.

Preparation

EXERCISE 1

Obtain several pieces of 9" x 12" yellow construction paper. Find an emoticon (those smiley-face drawings that express various types of emotions) chart online. Draw a replica of a different emoticon on each of the pieces of yellow construction paper. Make enough for half the number of the members in the group. On separate white slips of paper (approximately 3" x 9"), write the word that describes each emoticon that you have drawn.

EXERCISE 2

Do you know of a group member who has a flair for the dramatic? Or perhaps you could do a dramatic reading. Have that person (or you) prepare a dramatic reading of either Psalm 6 or Psalm 13, emphasizing the emotions that are expressed in the psalm.

DISCUSSION

Familiarize yourself with the discussion questions included in the following "Group Participation" section, or choose which questions in this week's study you want to discuss with the group.

Group Participation

EXERCISE 1

As group members enter, give each person either one emoticon drawing or one slip of paper with the description. After everyone has arrived, ask them to go around the room and find the emoticon and the description that go together. Have each pair sit down as they find their match. After everyone has found a match, invite the pairs to discuss with each other what kinds of things cause them to feel this particular emotion. Invite them to share what happens when they have expressed that emotion. For example:

1. Do they feel that others validate or criticize that emotional reaction?
2. What are some appropriate ways to express that emotion?
3. What are inappropriate ways to express this emotion?
4. What is an appropriate response to someone who is expressing this emotion?
5. How do they want to be treated when they are feeling emotional?

EXERCISE 2

Share the prepared dramatic reading of Psalm 6 or 13. After the presentation, discuss the following:

1. Who is expressing these emotions? (*King David*)
2. What do you know of David's life that would explain these emotions that are expressed? (*David was chosen to be king after Saul, and because of that Saul hated him and pursued him in order to kill him. David had other enemies who wanted to destroy him as well.*)
3. What do you learn from David's expression of his raw emotions in this psalm?
4. What does this teach you about how to express your emotions to God?
5. How does the psalm end? (*With assurance that God has heard and answered, a change of attitude, peace.*)
6. Have you ever had a similar experience where life was difficult and you raged at the Lord, but He changed your attitude and brought you peace?

DISCUSSION

1. Invite a volunteer to read the statements about emotions in the "A Closer Look at the Problem" section on pages 63-64. Ask group members to discuss what they think about these statements. Do they agree or disagree with each statement? Is there anything else they have learned about emotions that could be added to this list?

2. Discuss the following questions (or the ones you chose) from the "A Closer Look at God's Truth" section:

   · The healthiest way to handle emotions is to say "I am feeling angry" instead of "You make me angry." Which do you usually say?

   · Read Ephesians 4:26-27. What does Paul tell us is the greatest danger we face when we have negative feelings toward another person?

   · Recall some times in your life when you held on to your anger and resentment and did not forgive the person who hurt you until days, weeks, months or years after the day of the emotional event. In what ways, if any, did the devil gain a foothold over your life during that time?

   · Read Exodus 20:5 and Numbers 11:10. What are the two negative emotions God feels?

   · How do you want to be treated when you're emotionally upset?

ADDITIONAL DISCUSSION/ACTION STEPS

1. Have the members share if they ever judge themselves as less of a Christian because of what they feel. If so, what will they apply from this lesson?

2. Have the group share what difficulties they have in accepting their emotional makeup as God's good gift to them. What did they discover from this week's study about God's attitude toward emotions?

3. Ask the members whether criticism, correction or judgment is their usual response to the emotions of others. What will they apply from

this week's lesson to help them listen to others without responding in these negative ways?

SEVEN

LEARNING TO LISTEN

Objective

To give group members opportunities to practice their listening skills.

Preparation

EXERCISE 1
Arrange the chairs in the meeting room in a horseshoe shape.

EXERCISE 2
Obtain half sheets of paper and pens or pencils. Prepare a short story that only takes a couple of minutes to read. An appropriate story would have some details that can be questioned later. Prepare five to six questions related to the details of the story (for example, What color was the car? How many people were in the story? What was the occupation of the person in the story?)

Discussion

Familiarize yourself with the discussion questions included in the following "Group Participation" section, or choose which questions in this week's study you want to discuss with the group.

Group Participation

EXERCISE 1
Play a game of Telephone (sometimes called Gossip). Arrange chairs in a horseshoe shape. When everyone is seated, whisper a statement to the first person next to you and ask him or her to whisper the same statement to the next person until the statement has reached the last person. Ask the

last person to repeat the statement that he or she has heard. You will undoubtedly get a different version of the initial statement. At the conclusion of the game, discuss the following:

1. Why does the statement change as it goes from one person to another? (*Not listening carefully, distractions or other noises, not speaking clearly.*)

2. Why do we have trouble listening attentively to others? (*We are thinking of what we want to say, our minds wander, self-centeredness, and so forth.*)

EXERCISE 2
Read the short story, instructing the group members to listen carefully. When you complete the story, hand out the paper and pens or pencils. Instruct the members to write the numbers 1 to 5 (or 1 to 6) down the side of the paper. Tell them you will ask some questions about the story and they will write their answers. When you have asked the questions, invite members to share their answers. Correct any wrong answers. Then discuss what kinds of things keep us from remembering what we hear.

DISCUSSION
1. Discuss the following questions (or the ones you chose) from the "A Closer Look at God's Truth" section:

  • Read Luke 15:18-20. Before reaching his father's home, the prodigal son had carefully planned and practiced what he would say to his father. What approach was he going to take?

  • Read Matthew 5:23-24. What premium does God place on reconciliation?

  • If you procrastinate in asking for forgiveness, what additional problems might you create for yourself?

  • What do Proverbs 18:13 and James 1:19 have to say about listening?

  • What character weaknesses might our tongue reveal about ourselves?

2. Discuss the following questions from the "A Closer Look at My Own Heart" section:

    •   Describe a time when you put self-protection above the pain you caused another person.

    •   When was the last time you said to someone, "I was wrong. I need you to forgive me"? How difficult was it to say? What was the outcome?

    •   What prevents you from saying "Forgive me" more often?

ADDITIONAL DISCUSSION/ACTION STEPS

1. Ask the group members what they learned about listening from this week's lesson.

2. Have the participants relate some of the things they need to put into practice to improve their listening skills this week.

EIGHT

GROWING IN GRACE

Objective

To help group members understand the power of grace in healing their relationships with others.

Preparation

EXERCISE 1

Prepare two charts using poster board to illustrate "the Upward and Downward Spirals of Life" (see pages 91-92). Draw the spirals and list the items beside them in order as they appear in the book.

EXERCISE 2

Invite someone—preferably one of the group members—to lead the group in singing two or three praise and worship songs. Or obtain a worship CD and a CD player. This will be used at the end of the session.

DISCUSSION

Familiarize yourself with the discussion questions included in the following "Group Participation" section, or choose which questions in this week's study you want to discuss with the group. Note that if you choose to do exercise 2 above, you will want to leave about 10 minutes at the end of the session for a time of praise and worship, so choose just the number of questions that you think your group will be able to discuss during the meeting time.

Group Participation

EXERCISE 1

Display the two charts that you made side by side. Invite the group members to make observations about these illustrations. Invite them to share examples of how they have seen either one of these charts illustrated in their own relationships. Briefly discuss how "replacement thinking" can help in restoring a relationship and how keeping this chart in mind can help them when a relationship is descending into brokenness.

DISCUSSION

1. Discuss the following lies and the biblical truths that counteract those lies from the "A Closer Look at God's Truth" section, and have members share how they wrote the truth after reading the Scriptures:

   - *The Lie:* When people act unfairly, unkindly, thoughtlessly or obnoxiously, I should blame them and dwell on the wrong done to me or to others.
   - *The Truth:* (Using Romans 12:14,17-18 and Ephesians 4:31-32)

   - *The Lie:* When I am rejected, hurt or unfairly treated, I have a right to be in a bad mood and harbor negative thoughts.
   - *The Truth:* (Using Matthew 5:11-12)

   - *The Lie:* I have a right to criticize and judge other Christians when they fail to obey God's laws. When they don't, I should be depressed.
   - *The Truth:* (Using Matthew 7:1-5 and Galatians 6:1-2)

   - *The Lie:* I have a right to expect people to remember me, give me gifts and do special things for me. When they don't, I should be depressed.
   - *The Truth:* (Using Philippians 2:3)

   - *The Lie:* I expect people to listen to what's on my mind.
   - *The Truth:* (Using James 1:19,26)

2. If you choose to do exercise 1 (and time allows), discuss any of the following additional questions from the "A Closer Look at God's Truth" section:

   - Read Philippians 4:8. List the things Christians are called to think about.

- If you produce emotional home movies in your mind or lose sleep over your late-night shows, what can you do to stop the negative, get-even thinking?

- Read Psalm 42:1-3 and list the emotions that David was feeling.

- Read Psalm 42:9-10 and describe David's attitude toward God.

- Read Psalm 42:4-6 and list what David chose to think about, even in his depressed emotional state.

3. If you did not choose to do exercise 1 (and time allows), have participants refer to "The Upward and Downward Spirals of Life" charts on page 91-92 and discuss the following questions:

- Study the upward and downward spirals. Where do you see victory in your life?

- Where do you see defeat?

- Pinpoint the step that causes you to stumble into a downward spiral.

- Have you let a relationship grow cool because you were hurt? Based on this lesson, what steps will you take to try to restore the relationship with the one who hurt you?

ADDITIONAL DISCUSSION/ACTION STEPS
Ask if anyone completed the relationship worksheet at the end of the chapter. Invite volunteers to share the results, cautioning them to not mention specific names or relationships in their sharing.

EXERCISE 2
Close this final session with a time of praise and worship. Begin with a time of group prayer, asking the Lord to help us heal any broken relationships. Conclude by singing praise and worship songs.

What Is Aglow International?

―――∽✺∾―――

From one nation to 172 worldwide...
From one fellowship to more than 4,600...
From 100 people to more than 17 million...

Aglow International has experienced phenomenal growth since
its inception 40 years ago. In 1967, four women from the state
of Washington prayed for a way to reach out to other Christian
women in simple fellowship, free from denominational boundaries.

―∽∾―

The first meeting held in Seattle, Washington, USA, drew more
than 100 women to a local hotel. From that modest beginning,
Aglow International has become one of the largest intercultural,
interdenominational women's organizations in the world.

―∽∾―

Each year, an estimated 17 million people are ministered to
through Aglow's local fellowship meetings, Bible studies, support
groups, retreats, conferences and various outreaches. From the
inner city to the upper echelons, from the woman next door to
the corporate executive, Aglow seeks to minister to the felt
needs of women around the world.

―∽∾―

Christian women find Aglow a "safe place" to grow spiritually
and begin to discover and use the gifts, talents and abilities God
has given them. Aglow offers excellent leadership training and
varied opportunities to develop those leadership skills.

―∽∾―

Undergirding the evangelistic thrust of the ministry is an emphasis on prayer, which has led to an active prayer network linking
six continents. The vast prayer power available through Aglow
women around the world is being used by God to influence
countless lives in families, communities, cities and nations.

Aglow's Mission Statement

Our mission is to lead women to Jesus Christ and provide opportunity for Christian women to grow in their faith and minister to others.

———

Aglow's Continuing Focus...

- To reconcile a woman to her womanhood as God designed. To strengthen and empower her to fulfill the unfolding plan of God as He brings restoration to the male/female relationship, which is the foundation of the home, the church and the community.
- To love women of all cultures, with a special focus on Muslim women.
- To reach out to every strata of society, from inner cities to isolated outposts to our own neighborhoods, with very practical and tangible expressions of the love of Jesus.

———

Aglow Ministers In...

Albania, Angola, Anguilla, Antigua, Argentina, Aruba, Australia, Austria, Bahamas, Bahrain, Barbados, Belarus, Belgium, Belize, Benin, Bermuda, Bolivia, Botswana, Brazil, Britain, Bulgaria, Burkina Faso, Cameroon, Canada, Chile, China, Colombia, Congo (Dem. Rep. of), Congo (Rep. of), Costa Rica, Côte d'Ivoire, Cuba, Curaçao, Czech Republic, Denmark, Djibouti, Dominica, Dominican Republic, Ecuador, Egypt, El Salvador, Equatorial Guinea, Estonia, Ethiopia, Faroe Islands, Fiji, Finland, France, Gabon, the Gambia, Germany, Ghana, Grand Cayman, Greece, Grenada, Guam, Guatemala, Guinea, Guyana, Haiti, Honduras, Hungary, Iceland, India, Indonesia, Ireland, Israel, Jamaica, Japan, Kazakstan, Kenya, Korea, Kyrgyzstan, Latvia, Lithuania, Malawi, Malaysia, Mali, Mauritius, Mexico, Mongolia, Mozambique, Myanmar, Nepal, Netherlands, New Zealand, Nicaragua, Niger, Nigeria, Norway, Oman, Pakistan, Panama, Papua New Guinea, Peru, Philippines, Portugal, Puerto Rico, Romania, Russia, Rwanda, Samoa, Samoa (American), Scotland, Senegal, Serbia, Sierra Leone, Singapore, South Africa, Spain, Sri Lanka, St. Kitts, St. Lucia, St. Maarten, St. Vincent, Sudan, Suriname, Sweden, Switzerland, Tajikistan, Tanzania, Thailand, Togo, Tonga, Trinidad/ Tobago, Turks & Caicos Islands, Uganda, Ukraine, United States, Uruguay, Uzbekistan, Venezuela, Vietnam, Virgin Islands (American), Virgin Islands (British), Wales, Yugoslavia, Zambia, Zimbabwe, and other nations.

How do I find my nearest Aglow Fellowship? Call or write us at:

AGLOW
INTERNATIONAL

P.O. Box 1749, Edmonds, WA 98020-1749
Phone: 425-775-7282 or 1-800-793-8126
Fax: 425-778-9615   E-mail: aglow@aglow.org
Web site: http://www.aglow.org/

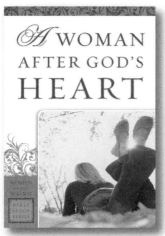
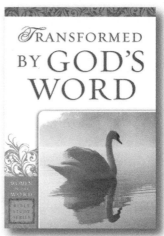